Nikon Coolpix p1000 User Companion

Your Indispensable Handbook with Illustrations to Master the p1000

By

Mats Sauer

Table of Content

INTRODUCTION

The Nikon Coolpix P1000 is a superzoom bridge camera released in 2018. It is known for its incredible 125x optical zoom, which allows it to capture photos and videos of distant subjects with incredible detail. The P1000 is also equipped with various other features that make it a versatile and powerful camera, including a high-resolution electronic viewfinder, Dual Detect Optical VR image stabilization, and 4K UHD video recording.

A bridge camera is a digital camera between a point-and-shoot camera and a DSLR camera. It has a larger sensor and lens than a point-and-shoot camera, but it is still relatively compact and easy to use. Bridge cameras are a good choice for photographers who want more control over their images than a point-and-shoot camera can offer but who want to avoid the size and weight of a DSLR camera.

The P1000's 125x optical zoom is its most impressive feature. It lets the camera capture photos and videos of distant subjects with incredible detail. For example, the P1000 can take close-up photos of birds and wildlife, even if they are miles away. It can also photograph celestial objects such as the moon and planets.

The P1000 is a unique camera that offers photographers unprecedented reach and flexibility. With its incredible zoom range, it can capture everything from wide-angle landscapes to close-up portraits of distant subjects. It is also ideal for wildlife photography, astrophotography, and sports photography. The P1000 is not without its drawbacks. It is a large and heavy camera, and its zoom lens can be slow to focus. However, its benefits far outweigh its drawbacks, making it a must-have camera for any photographer who wants to capture any subject, no matter how far away it is.

The P1000 is the perfect camera for photographers who want to capture distant subjects, such as birds, wildlife, and celestial objects. It is also an excellent camera for sports and travel photography.

In this book, we will teach you everything you need to know about using the Nikon Coolpix P1000 to take amazing photos. We will cover everything from basic camera settings to advanced techniques.

Chapter 1: Getting The Camera Up and Running

Preparing the Camera for Initial Use

Attaching Strap

Nikon, a household name in the camera industry for over a century, has a history of pushing boundaries and creating world-renowned cameras. One of Nikon's most popular cameras, the Coolpix P1000, has been in production for almost a decade, yet it remains a formidable contender. Its impressive features and Nikon's commitment to longevity are a testament to the brand's excellence.

Although it is easy to find a strap for the Nikon Coolpix P1000, finding one that fits properly can be challenging. This section will show you how to attach the strap that comes with the camera. The P1000 can also be attached to almost any tripod using its standard tripod mount. Even when using a tripod or other stabilizer, the camera's built-in image stabilization can help keep shots steady.

This camera has various colorful and durable strap options that can be attached quickly and easily. No special tools or skills are required. To attach a strap, simply follow these steps:

Step 1: Slide the battery compartment door up and open it.

Step 2: Remove the battery from the camera by sliding it down and out through the gap in the bottom of the camera. Replace the battery with the new one.

Step 3: Insert one end of the new strap into the hole at one end of the camera's mount and press down until you hear a click. It will secure the strap in place so it cannot fall out.

Step 4: Attach the other end of the new strap to a different camera mounting point on the body.

Step 5: Close both ends of the new strap together until you hear a click. It will secure the strap in place.

Attaching lens cap

Before replacing the sensor on the Nikon Coolpix P1000, please turn off the camera and disconnect it from the power source.

Flip the camera over and find the metal tab behind the lens cover. Use your thumb or a small flat-head screwdriver to pry the tab out of its socket.

Flip the camera back over and find the plastic piece covering the socket where you just pried out the metal tab. Use your thumb or a small flat-head screwdriver to remove the plastic piece.

Remove the remaining screws from the other plastic pieces that cover up other sockets.

Use your thumb or a small flat-head screwdriver to remove the front of the camera.

Remove the screws from the other side of the small white circuit board revealed in the previous step. Carefully pry off the tiny plastic pieces surrounding the board until it is exposed enough to remove with your fingers or by using your thumbs and index fingers together.

Pull away the white circuit board to get a good grip on it. Use your thumb or a small flat-head screwdriver to lift the remaining plastic pieces from around the white circuit board. Finally, remove the white circuit board from its socket in the camera body by reaching into the gap with your finger or thumb.

Carefully pull on the plastic parts until they are all gone, revealing a small black chip with two opposing sides tipped with gold-colored contacts.

Use your thumb and fingers to remove the black chip from its socket on the circuit board. Replace the chip and make sure it is firmly in place. Use your other hand to re-attach the plastic pieces from step 9 that were removed to hide this chip.

Attaching lens hood

A lens hood is an essential accessory for any camera. It is attached to the front of the lens to protect it from dust, debris, and unwanted light. It can reduce lens flare and improve the overall image quality.

Wide-angle lenses with large front elements often come with lens hoods, but standard lenses and telescopes can also benefit from them.

The Nikon Coolpix P1000 has a built-in lens hood, which is easy to attach and remove. However, some photographers prefer a dedicated lens hood to protect their expensive equipment.

Inserting/removing battery

Inserting battery

Changing the batteries in a Nikon Coolpix P1000 is very easy. To access the battery compartment, remove the two screws from the camera's underside and pull it out.

It is essential to replace dead batteries promptly, especially if you plan on taking photos while on vacation or a trip. Otherwise, you may miss out on capturing important moments.

Here's how to install a battery in the Nikon Coolpix P1000:

1. Eject the memory card from your camera.
2. Press down and pull out the battery cover.
3. Replace the battery with the positive side facing up.

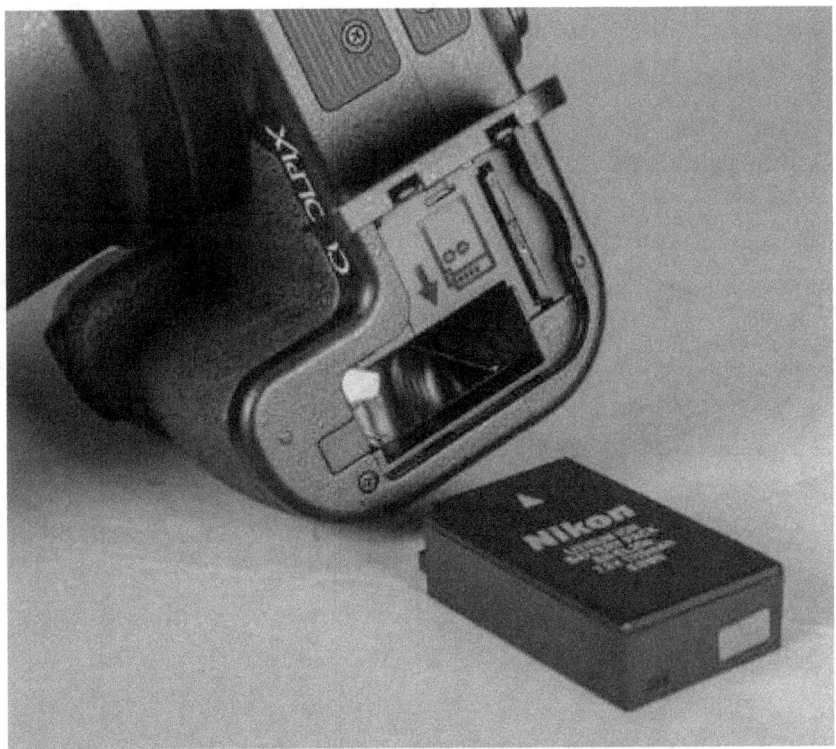

4. Insert the memory card back into the slot and close the door.
5. Turn on the camera by pressing the power button.

Removing battery

The Nikon Coolpix P1000's battery is relatively easy to remove due to its awkward placement in the camera. The battery compartment is located on the camera's underside and is accessible by removing two screws. However, there is very little space to work with, and the battery is tightly wedged in place. It makes it easier to remove the battery with a tool, such as a small screwdriver or coin.

11

Despite this inconvenience, the Nikon Coolpix P1000 is widely regarded as one of Nikon's best compact cameras. It has a powerful zoom lens and various advanced features, making it a popular choice for photographers of all levels.

Here's how you can access and remove the battery from your Nikon Coolpix P1000

1. Pull the battery cover towards you and slowly release it to remove it.
2. Slide the battery connection out of the camera's battery slot and remove the battery.
3. Please insert the new battery into the camera and push it back in until you hear a click.
4. Carefully position the battery cover over the new battery and push it toward the camera's front until it latches.

Inserting/removing memory card

Inserting memory card

To insert a memory card into the Nikon Coolpix P1000:

1. Flip open the camera's rear cover.
2. Locate the memory card slot on the left side of the camera body.
3. Push the lever next to the memory card slot towards you until it clicks into place.
4. Insert the memory card into the slot until it clicks into place.

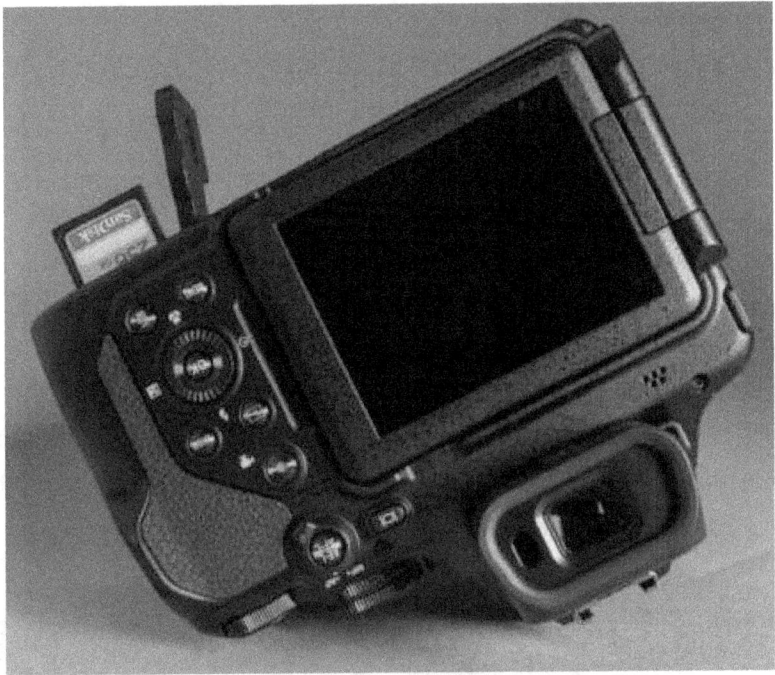

5. Close the memory card slot cover.
6. Close the camera's rear cover.

Removing memory card

Removing the memory card from your camera safely is essential to avoid losing your data, such as images and preferences. The process is simple, but if you have never done it before, it can be unclear.

To remove the memory card from your camera safely:

1. Turn off the camera and disconnect the power source.
2. Remove the back cover.
3. Use a brush or cloth to clean the camera's exterior.
4. Locate the latch on the memory card slot and unlock it.

5. Gently pull out the memory card.
6. Place the memory card in an anti-static bag and then place the bag in a resealable plastic bag.
7. Label the bag with your name, the date, and a summary of the contents.
8. Insert the new memory card into the slot.

Charging battery

The Nikon Coolpix P1000 has a wide ISO range (from 100 to 12800), making it ideal for low-light photography. Its anti-shake feature also helps to capture sharp images, even when the subject is moving quickly.

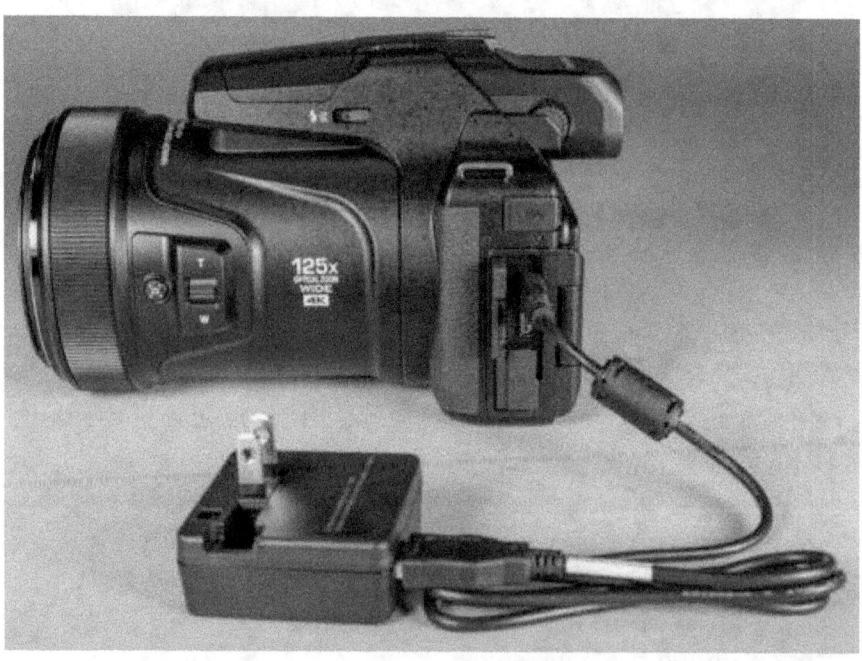

However, the Nikon Coolpix P1000 does not have a removable battery, so you need to be mindful of where you store it until you are ready to use it. Nevertheless, the battery life of the Nikon Coolpix P1000 is excellent, making it a great choice if you need a camera that can last all day long.

Setting the Date, Time, and Language

Set the date and time on your camera before you start taking pictures. The camera will save this information (also known as metadata) with each image, and you can view it later if you want. One day, you'll be glad you have the correct date and time recorded with your digital photos. Your camera will prompt you to set the date and time you first turn it on.

To set the date and time later, turn on the camera by pressing and holding the power button. Then, press the Menu button below the OK button on the back. Finally, press the left button, marked with a timer icon.

When you press the left button, a yellow highlight will appear on the left side of the screen over a list of icons. The top icon represents the camera's current mode, such as P for Program, an icon for Bird-watching or Moon if the camera is in shooting mode, or a triangle icon for playback mode if the camera is in playback mode.

Use the down button, marked with a flower icon, to move the yellow highlight to the wrench icon, which represents the Setup menu.

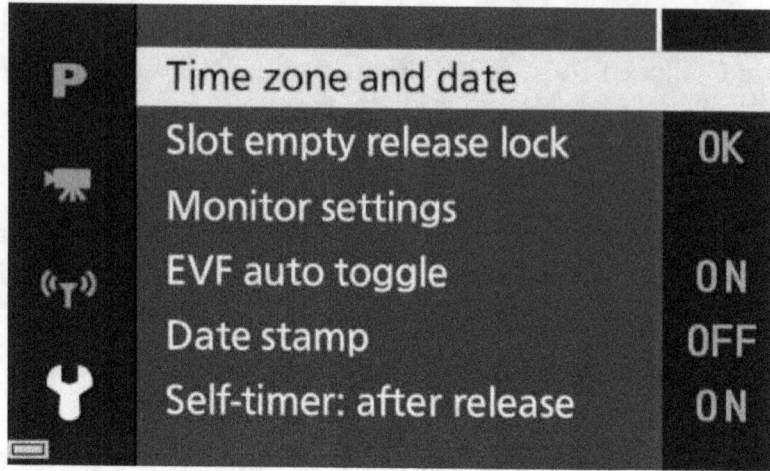

Press the right button, marked with a plus and minus sign, to move the yellow highlight back to the right, where it will highlight a menu item. Press the up and down buttons (or rotate the multi-selector dial) to move the yellow highlight to the Time Zone and Date line, and press the OK button to open a screen with choices of Sync with Smart Device, Date and Time, Date Format, and Time Zone.

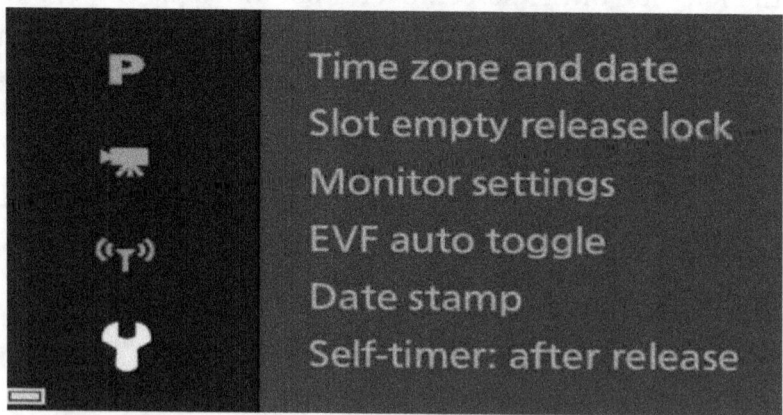

To open the date and time settings, highlight Date and Time and press OK. You can also press the right button to move to these menu screens.

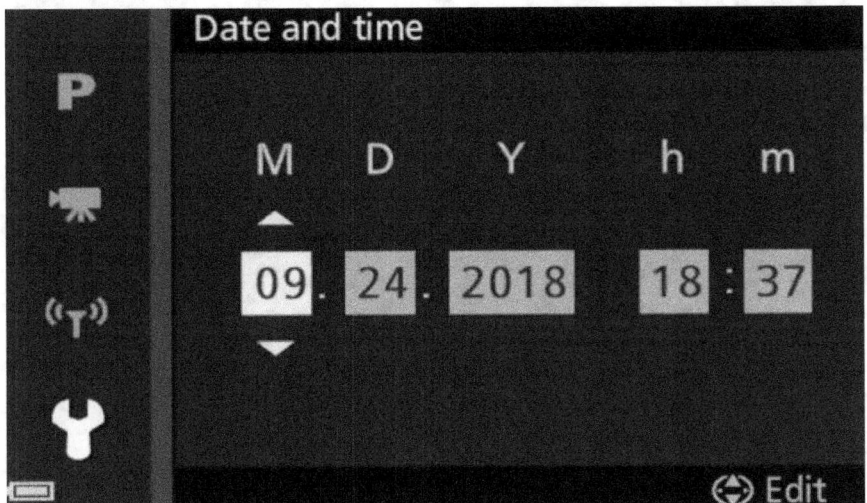

On the settings screen, use the left and right buttons to navigate through the date, year, and time settings. Change the settings by pressing the up and down buttons or by turning the multi-selector dial or command dial. When finished, press OK to confirm and Menu to exit the menu system.

To change the language of the camera menus and messages, go to the Language menu item on the third screen of the Setup menu. You can do this by pressing the right button or the OK button. Then, use the up and down buttons (or the multi-selector dial) to scroll to the language of your choice, and press the OK button to select it.

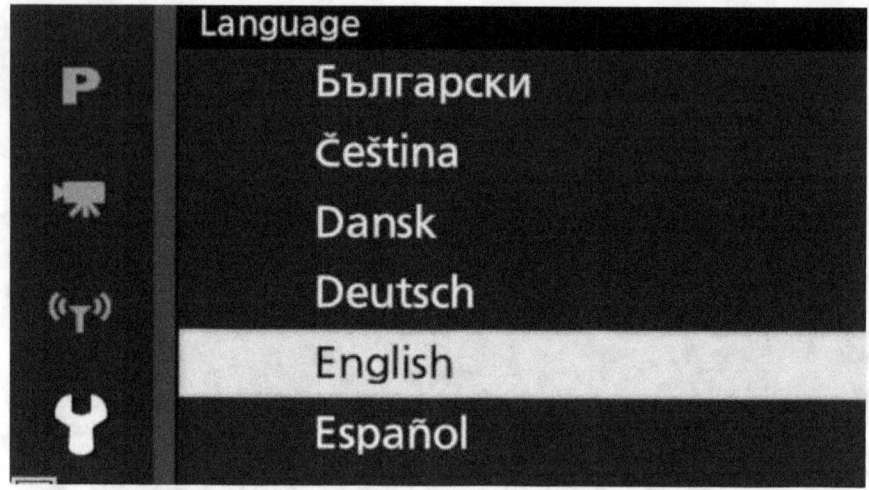

Then, press Menu to exit the menu system.

Exploring External Camera Features

Topside controls

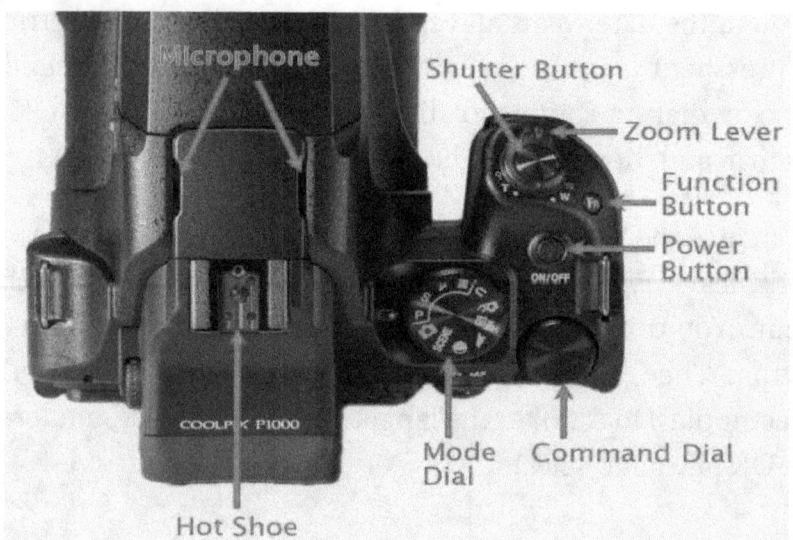

Hot shoe: The hot shoe is used to attach an external flash unit to the camera. This can be useful for using more powerful flashes or for using flashes that offer more features than the built-in flash.

Microphone: The microphone is used to record audio for video recordings. It is also used by the camera's autofocus system to detect the sound of voices, which can help to improve autofocus performance.

Shutter button: The shutter button is used to take pictures. When you press the shutter button halfway, the camera will focus on the subject. When you press the button all the way down, the camera will take a picture.

Zoom lever: The zoom lever is used to zoom the lens in and out. To zoom the lens in, push the lever forward. To zoom the lens out, pull the lever back.

Mode dial: The mode dial is used to select the camera's shooting mode. The available shooting modes include:

- Auto: The camera automatically selects the best settings for the current scene.
- Programmed Auto: This mode allows you to adjust some of the camera's settings, such as exposure compensation and white balance.
- Shutter Priority: This mode allows you to set the shutter speed, while the camera automatically selects the aperture.

- Aperture Priority: This mode allows you to set the aperture, while the camera automatically selects the shutter speed.
- Manual: This mode allows you to manually set both the shutter speed and aperture.

Command dial: The command dial is used to adjust various camera settings, depending on the mode that the camera is in. For example, in aperture priority mode, the command dial can be used to adjust the aperture. In shutter priority mode, the command dial can be used to adjust the shutter speed. And in manual mode, the command dial can be used to adjust the aperture, shutter speed, or ISO.

Power button: The power button is used to turn the camera on and off.

Function button: The function button can be used to access various camera settings quickly. The specific settings that are accessed will depend on the mode that the camera is in.

Front features

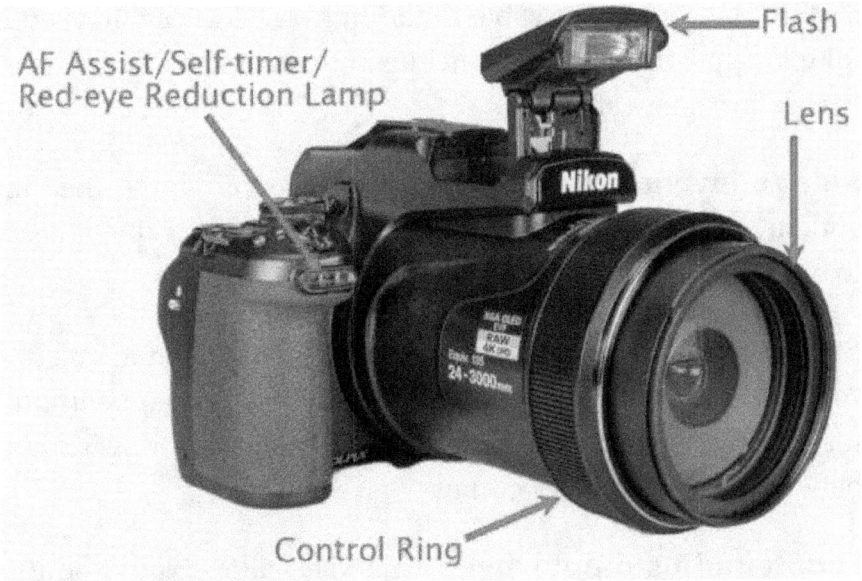

Flash

AF Assist/Self-timer/
Red-eye Reduction Lamp

Lens

Control Ring

Flash pop-up switch: This switch is used to raise and lower the built-in flash. The flash can be used to provide additional light in low-light situations or to fill in shadows.

Microphone jack: This jack allows you to connect an external microphone to the camera. This can be useful for recording audio in noisy environments or for capturing better quality audio for video recordings.

USB and HDMI ports: The USB port can be used to connect the camera to a computer to transfer files or to update the camera's firmware. The HDMI port can be used to connect the camera to an external monitor or TV to view your images and videos on a larger screen.

Remote terminal: This terminal allows you to connect a remote shutter release cable to the camera. This can be useful for taking pictures without touching the camera, which can help to reduce camera shake.

Side zoom control: This lever allows you to zoom the lens in and out. It is located on the side of the camera, making it easy to operate with one hand.

Snap-back zoom button: This button allows you to quickly zoom the lens out to its widest focal length. This can be useful for quickly finding your subject in the frame or for switching between different compositions.

Diopter adjustment wheel: This wheel allows you to adjust the focus of the viewfinder to match your eyesight. This is important for ensuring that you can clearly see the image through the viewfinder before you take a picture.

Control ring: This ring allows you to quickly adjust various camera settings, such as aperture, shutter speed, and ISO. This can be useful for making quick adjustments to your camera settings without having to go into the menu system.

Flash: The built-in flash can be used to provide additional light in low-light situations or to fill in shadows. It can also be used to create special effects, such as red-eye reduction and catchlight.

Lens: The Nikon Coolpix P1000 features a 125x optical zoom lens with a focal length of 24-3000mm (equivalent). This makes it possible to capture distant subjects with great detail or to zoom in on small details.

AF assist/ Self-timer/ Red-eye reduction lamp: This lamp is used to assist the autofocus system in low-light conditions. It can also be used as a self-timer lamp or as a red-eye reduction lamp.

Back-of-the-body controls

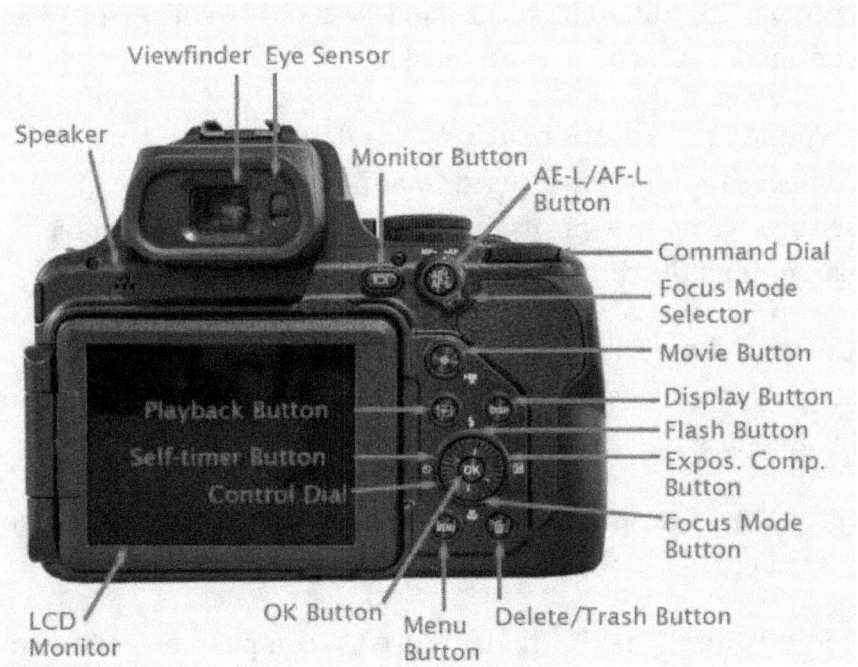

LCD monitor: The LCD monitor is used to view the image that you are composing, to view your images and videos after you have taken them, and to access the camera's menu system.

OK button: The OK button is used to confirm your selections in the menu system and to accept changes to camera settings.

Menu button: The menu button is used to open the camera's menu system.

Delete/Trash button: The delete/trash button is used to delete images and videos from the camera's memory card.

Focus mode button: The focus mode button is used to toggle between the different focus modes, such as single-shot AF, continuous AF, and manual focus.

Exposure compensation button: The exposure compensation button is used to adjust the camera's exposure settings. This can be useful for making images brighter or darker than the camera would normally expose them.

Control dial: The control dial is used to adjust various camera settings, such as aperture, shutter speed, and ISO. It can also be used to scroll through the camera's menu system.

Speaker: The speaker is used to play back audio from video recordings.

Viewfinder: The viewfinder is used to compose images and to view images and videos without having to use the LCD monitor.

Eye sensor: The eye sensor automatically switches the camera between the viewfinder and the LCD monitor when you bring your eye to the viewfinder.

Monitor button: The monitor button is used to toggle the display on the LCD monitor.

Self-timer button: The self-timer button is used to delay the shutter release by a few seconds. This can be useful for taking self-portraits or group photos.

Playback button: The playback button is used to enter playback mode, where you can view your images and videos.

AE-L/AF-L button: The AE-L/AF-L button is used to lock the exposure and autofocus settings. This can be useful for preventing the camera from changing these settings while you are composing an image.

Command dial: The command dial is used to adjust various camera settings, such as aperture, shutter speed, and ISO. It can also be used to scroll through the camera's menu system.

Focus mode selector: The focus mode selector is used to manually select the focus mode.

Movie button: The movie button is used to start and stop video recording.

Display button: The display button is used to change the information that is displayed on the LCD monitor.

Flash button: The flash button is used to toggle the flash between on, off, and auto modes.

Working with Memory Cards

Press the MENU button > Setting menu icon > Format card > OK button

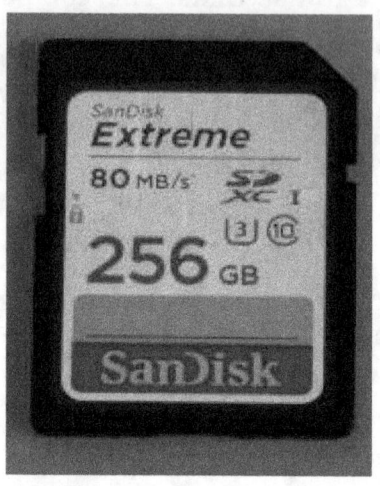

Use this option to format a memory card. Formatting a memory card will permanently delete all data on the card. This data cannot be recovered. Be sure to back up any important images on a computer before formatting.

To format the memory card, select Format on the screen and press the OK button.

Do not turn off the camera or open the battery chamber/memory card slot cover while formatting the memory card.

This setting may not be available while a wireless connection is active.

CHAPTER 2: CHOOSING BASIC PICTURE SETTINGS

Choosing Shooting Mode

Like other sophisticated digital cameras, the Nikon Coolpix P1000 has many settings, especially for still photography. This book aims to provide clear guidance on these features. To start, let's look at the P1000's multiple shooting modes, which give you many options for your photography.

To take still images with the Nikon Coolpix P1000, you can choose from a variety of shooting modes, including Auto, Program, Shutter Priority, Aperture Priority, Manual exposure, User Settings, Creative, Bird-watching, Moon, and Scene. (There is also a Movie Manual mode for movies only.)

Auto Mode

The Auto-shooting mode is a good choice for quick shots, such as in fast-paced environments where you don't have time to adjust settings. The camera will automatically select the best settings for the scene so you can focus on taking the photo.

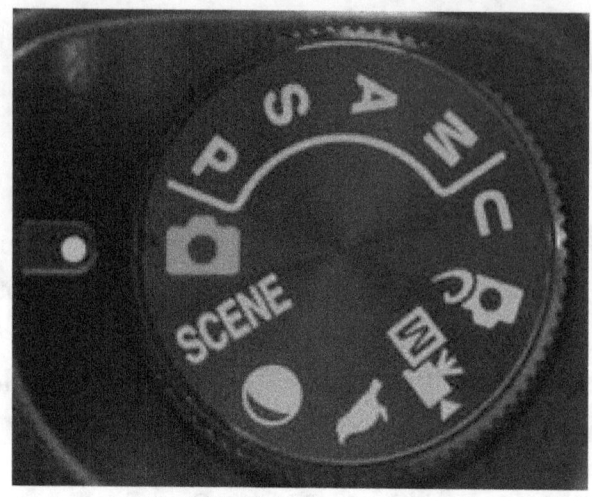

For example, I used this mode to grab a shot of a couple on a pedestrian bridge over the James River. In this shooting mode, the camera will detect human faces and focus on them if possible, but it does not try to figure out what kind of scene it is photographing.

To set Auto mode on the Nikon Coolpix P1000, turn the mode dial, located on the top of the camera to the right of the viewfinder, to the green camera icon.

Auto mode on the Nikon Coolpix P1000 is a convenient way to take quick photos, but it limits your creative control. In Auto mode, the camera automatically selects the ISO, white balance, metering method, and Picture Control settings. You also cannot select continuous shooting.

If you want more control over your photos, you can use one of the other shooting modes, such as Program, Shutter Priority,

Aperture Priority, or Manual. These modes give you more flexibility to adjust the camera's settings to your liking.

Even in Auto mode, you can still control some settings on the Nikon Coolpix P1000. For example, you can choose the image size and quality, use exposure compensation, and select a flash mode. You can also select macro, infinity, or manual focus and use the self-timer and smile timer options. I recommend setting the image size to the maximum of 4608 x 3456 pixels and the image quality to Fine. You can use the other available settings as needed.

Program Mode

To choose Program mode, turn the mode dial to the P position.

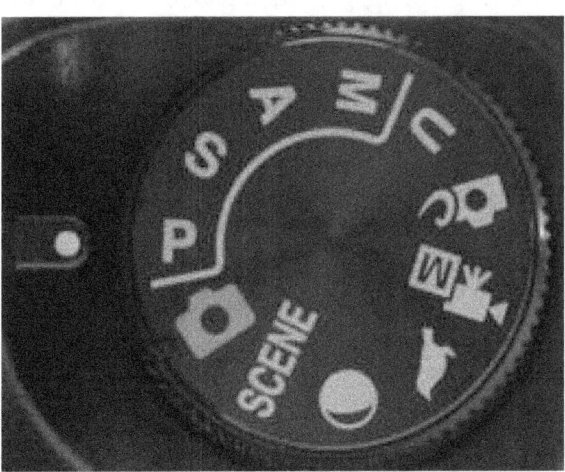

In Program mode, the camera automatically sets the shutter speed and aperture to produce a well-exposed photo. You can still control many other settings, such as ISO, white balance, and metering mode. You can also use exposure compensation to override the camera's automatic exposure.

Flexible program is a feature on Nikon cameras that allows you to adjust the shutter speed and aperture values that the camera selects in Program mode. It means that you can get more creative control over your photos without having to switch to a manual mode.

To use a flexible program, aim your camera at your subject and turn the command dial. The camera will display a list of equivalent shutter speeds and aperture combinations. You can then choose the combination that you want.

For example, if the camera selects 1/60 second at f/4.5, you could use a flexible program to choose 1/50 second at f/5.0, 1/40 second at f/5.6, or 1/30 second at f/6.3. These combinations will all result in the same exposure, but they will have different effects on the depth of field and motion blur.

A flexible program is a helpful feature for photographers who want more creative control over their photos without having to learn about all of the manual settings. It is also an excellent way to learn about the relationship between shutter speed and aperture.

When you use a flexible program, the camera will display an asterisk (*) next to the P symbol in the top left corner of the screen. It means that the camera is using different settings than it would in normal Program mode. To cancel the flexible program, turn the command dial back to its original position, select a different shooting mode, or turn off the camera.

The flexible program feature is a great way to learn about photography and to experiment with different settings. It allows you to see what the camera's "normal" settings are and to try different combinations of aperture and shutter speed to see how they affect your photos.

For example, you can use a flexible program to create a blurred background or to stop motion. You can also use it to see how different settings affect the brightness and exposure of your photos. A flexible program is a free and easy way to experiment with different photography techniques. It is a great way to learn about your camera and to improve your photography skills.

Program mode gives you more control over your camera's settings than Auto mode. You can adjust settings such as white balance, ISO sensitivity, metering mode, autofocus mode, and continuous shooting.

Shutter Priority Mode

To select Shutter Priority mode on the Nikon Coolpix P1000, turn the mode dial to the S position.

In this mode, you can set the shutter speed, and the camera will automatically set the aperture to produce a well-exposed photo. It is helpful for situations where you want to control the amount of motion blur in your photos. For example, you might use a faster shutter speed to freeze motion in a sports photo or a slower shutter speed to create a blurred background in a portrait photo.

The camera has some built-in limitations on the shutter speeds that you can use. For example, the fastest shutter speed available is 1/4000 of a second, and the slowest shutter speed available is eight seconds. The camera will also automatically adjust the aperture based on the shutter speed that you select.

To freeze motion in your photos, you need to use a fast shutter speed. A fast shutter speed is also helpful in taking photos of subjects that are moving quickly, such as a baseball swing or a bird in flight. To create a blurred effect, such as a trail of car taillights at night, you need to use a slow shutter speed.

To set the shutter speed on the Nikon Coolpix P1000, turn the command dial, the ridged dial at the top right of the camera's back.

Once you have pressed the shutter button halfway, look at the shutter speed number on the screen. If the shutter speed number blinks, the camera cannot find an aperture setting that will produce a properly exposed photo. It can happen if the shutter speed is too fast or too slow for the current lighting conditions.

For example, if you try to use a shutter speed of two seconds in a well-lit room, the shutter speed number may blink because the camera cannot find an aperture setting that will produce a dark enough photo. If the shutter speed number is not blinking, the camera has found an aperture setting that will produce a properly exposed photo.

The camera lets you take the picture, even if the shutter speed number blinks. The camera wants to give you the creative freedom to take the photo you want, even if it means taking an overexposed or underexposed photo. It is less likely to happen in Aperture Priority mode because the camera has a wider range of shutter speeds.

When setting the shutter speed on your Nikon Coolpix P1000, the fractions of a second are displayed as standard fractions, such as 1/5 or 1/200. Longer shutter speeds are displayed using quotation marks, such as "1.3". The camera also displays some shutter speeds as fractions with decimal denominators, such as 1/1.3

Aperture Priority Mode

Aperture Priority mode (represented by the A setting on the mode dial) is the opposite of Shutter Priority mode.

In Aperture Priority mode, you choose the aperture, and the camera automatically chooses the shutter speed to produce a well-exposed photo. The shutter speed can range from 1/4000 of a second to eight seconds, depending on the ISO setting, aperture setting, and zoom position of the lens.

The camera's aperture is like the eye of the camera that can change its size to control how much light goes in. It's measured with numbers called f-stops. For the Coolpix P1000, it can go from letting in a lot of light (f/2.8) to very little light (f/8.0), but there are some limits. To make a picture, you adjust the aperture (how big the eye is) and the shutter speed (how long the eye stays open) to control the amount of light that comes in.

The aperture is the size of the opening in the camera lens that lets light in. The wider the aperture, the more light enters the camera, but the shallower the depth of field. The narrower the aperture, the less light enters the camera, but the deeper the depth of field. Depth of field is the range of distances in front of and behind the subject that are in focus. A shallow depth of field means that only a small range of distances is in focus while the rest of the image is blurred. A deep depth of field means that a large range of distances is in focus.

Imagine you are taking a photo of your friend standing 5 feet away from you. You want to blur the background so that your friend stands out. To do this, you would set a wide aperture, such as f/2.8. It will create a shallow depth of field, which will blur the background. If you want to keep everything in focus, including the background, you should set a narrow aperture, such as f/11. It will create a deep depth of field, keeping everything in focus.

The wider the camera's aperture, the more blurred the background will be. For example, if you are taking a portrait of someone with the aperture set to its widest opening, the background will be very blurred. The camera only focuses on the person in the foreground, and the background is out of focus. If you narrow the aperture, the background will become sharper. The camera now focuses on a wider range of distances.

It is difficult to blur the background in a photo taken with the Coolpix P1000 for two reasons:

The sensor in the Coolpix P1000 is small. A small sensor results in a deeper depth of field, which means that more of the scene will be in focus, even if you use a wide aperture.

The widest aperture available on the Coolpix P1000 is f/2.8. A wider aperture results in a shallower depth of field, which means that less of the scene will be in focus. Some compact cameras have lenses that open as wide as f/2.0 or even f/1.4, which makes it easier to blur the background.

The widest aperture available on the Coolpix P1000 is f/2.8, which is only available when the lens is zoomed out. As you zoom in, the widest aperture becomes smaller until it reaches f/8.0 at the maximum zoom range. It is challenging to design a lens that has a wide aperture at a long focal length. It is the reason why most telephoto lenses have relatively narrow apertures.

It isn't easy to show the difference between different apertures. Both photos were taken simultaneously and in the same place, with a model lighthouse in the foreground and a mannequin in the background. The lens was zoomed out to its widest setting, and the focus was on the model lighthouse in the foreground. The only difference between the two photos is the aperture setting. The first photo was taken at f/2.8, the widest possible setting and the second photo was taken at f/8.0, the narrowest possible setting.

The first photo (f/2.8) has a blurred background because the aperture is wide, and the depth of field is shallow. The second photo (f/8.0) has a sharper background because the aperture is narrow, and the depth of field is deep. If you want the sharpest picture possible, use a narrow aperture and zoom the lens back to its wide-angle setting. It will give you a deep depth of field, meaning everything in the scene will be in focus.

Photographers sometimes want to blur the background of a photo. It is called a shallow depth of field. It is often used in outdoor portraits to make the subject stand out. For example, if you are taking a photo of someone standing in front of a tree, you should blur the tree in the background so that the person is the only thing in focus. It will help the person stand out and make the photo visually appealing.

Manual Exposure Mode

The Coolpix P1000 has a mode that lets you control the aperture and shutter speed of the camera by hand. It means that you can choose the settings that you want instead of the camera choosing them for you.

It is helpful if you want to create a specific effect, such as a dark image. For example, the author of the paragraph used manual mode to take a dark photo of a conservatory. They experimented with different settings until they got the effect they wanted.

HDR (high dynamic range) images show a wide range of brightness levels, from very dark to very bright. It contrasts normal photos, which often have either overexposed (too bright) or underexposed (too dark) areas. One way to create HDR images is to take a series of photos at different exposures and then combine them using special software. It is called bracketing. To use manual mode on the Coolpix P1000, turn the mode dial to the M setting. Then, you will need to set the shutter speed and aperture yourself.

To set the shutter speed and aperture on the Coolpix P1000, look at the camera's display to find where they are displayed. The shutter speed is on the left, and the aperture is on the right. To set the shutter speed, turn the command dial (the wheel on the back of the camera, next to your thumb). To set the aperture, turn the multi-selector dial (the dial on the back of the camera, surrounding the OK button).

To change the shutter speed and aperture, turn the command and multi-selector dial, respectively. As you turn the dials, watch the vertical scale on the right side of the screen. The tick marks will turn yellow to show you the current settings.

The vertical scale on the right side of the screen shows how bright or dark the exposure will be. If the marks above the center of the scale turn yellow, the exposure will be too bright. If the marks below the center of the scale turn yellow, the exposure will be too dark. If the exposure is too bright or dark, the camera will show a yellow triangle at the top or bottom of the scale. /This means that the exposure is outside of the camera's range.

In dim light, it can be challenging to get a clear exposure without using a slow shutter speed. If you use a fast shutter speed, the image will be too dark. But if you use a slow shutter speed, the image will be blurry if you are not using a tripod.

In low light, you can adjust the exposure by increasing the ISO setting. The ISO setting controls how sensitive the camera's sensor is to light. A higher ISO setting means the sensor is more light-sensitive, so you can use a faster shutter speed and/or a narrower aperture without making the photo too dark.

In other shooting modes, the camera can automatically set the ISO setting to get a good exposure. But in manual mode, you need to set the ISO setting yourself. If you set the ISO setting to Auto in manual mode, the camera will set it to the lowest possible value, 100. The camera wants you to have complete control over the exposure.

If you are shooting in manual mode and need to increase the ISO setting, you can do so by going to the ISO Sensitivity item on the Shooting menu. You can choose any ISO value, including 400, 800, or even higher.

The exposure scale on the camera's display is a suggestion. You don't have to center the indicator on the scale to get good exposure. I suggest making the exposure darker or lighter than the camera suggests. Manual mode gives you complete control over the exposure of your photos. You can set the aperture and shutter speed independently, and the camera will not try to correct your settings.

The range of aperture and shutter speed settings available in manual mode changes depending on the focal length of the lens. The slowest shutter speeds, 15, 20, and 30 seconds, are only available in manual mode.

The slowest shutter speed available at a given ISO setting depends on the ISO setting. For example, the slowest shutter speed available at ISO 800 is 2 seconds, and the slowest shutter speed available at ISO 3200 is 1/2 second. If you set the ISO setting to Auto in manual mode, the camera will use an ISO setting of 100. The slowest shutter speeds are also available when ISO is set to Auto in manual mode only.

In manual mode, you can also use the Time and Bulb shutter speed settings, but only if you set the ISO to 100. With the Time setting, the shutter opens when you press the shutter button down all the way and closes when you press it down again.

With the Bulb setting, the shutter opens when you press the shutter button and stays open until you release it. The longest exposure you can take with either of these settings is 60 seconds. You cannot use continuous shooting with either setting. You cannot use the Auto Flash or Slow Sync flash modes in manual mode.

Setting Resolution and File Type (The Image Quality Setting)

Image Quality Setting

There are two basic settings to decide on your overall image "quality" in the broadest sense: Image Quality, discussed here, and Image Size, discussed below. The Image Quality option lets you select how much "compression" the camera applies. That is, the camera "compresses" the data by squeezing out a certain amount of information, preserving enough to recreate the image but trimming it down so the file does not take up too much storage space.

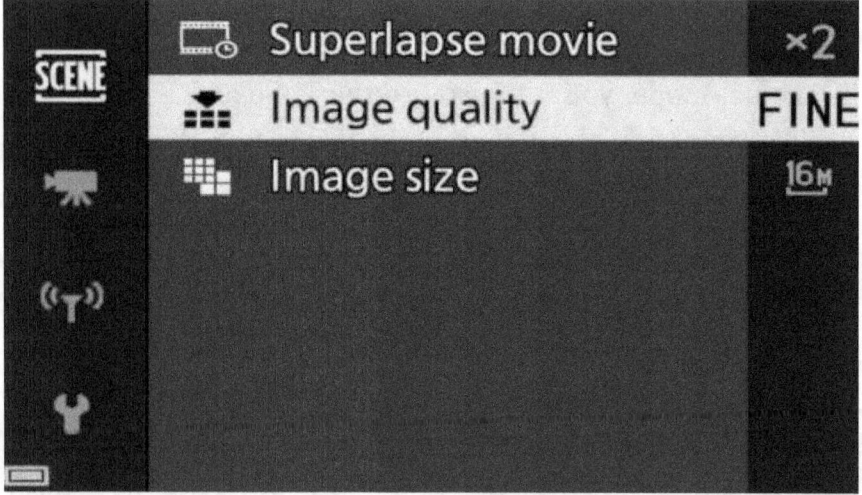

The two options are Fine and Normal. The Fine option uses roughly twice as much storage space as the Normal one. So, if you choose Fine for your quality setting, the camera can store about 3900 of the largest-sized images on a 32 GB memory card. If you choose Normal, it can store about 7800 of those images. Of course, there is a trade-off of quality against storage space. If you plan to make large prints or crop the image to use a portion of it, you should choose Fine.

It does not offer Raw as an option for image quality. Virtually all DSLRs and quite a few advanced compact cameras today offer the Raw format, which preserves the maximum image data and gives the user considerable flexibility in processing images in software. However, using Raw has disadvantages, including large file sizes and incompatibility with some post-processing software (at least until software updates are provided). Using a Raw format also requires that the images be processed in software; you cannot use them straight from the camera. The P1000 provides a great deal of flexibility in producing excellent JPEG (that is, compressed, non-Raw) images, and you should have no problem using this camera to make excellent prints or other photographic products.

Considering Resolution: Large, Medium, or Small?

The next option on the Shooting menu, Image Size, works hand-in-hand with Image Quality to determine the overall quality of your images. With the Coolpix P1000, Image Size has 2 components, which can be selected separately on some other cameras: resolution and aspect ratio. On the P1000, these 2 components are not named, but their numerical values are listed on the Image Size menu. (The aspect ratio values are listed only for the settings that deviate from the normal aspect ratio of 4:3.)

	Image size	
P	**16ᴹ**	**4608×3456**
	8ᴹ	3264×2448
	4ᴹ	2272×1704
((T))	2ᴹ	1600×1200
	16:9 12M	4608×2592
	3:2 14M	4608×3072

The image's resolution is the number of pixels it contains, given in a formula with the horizontal pixel count followed by the vertical pixel count. For example, the largest Image Size setting on the P1000 is 4608 x 3456, meaning the image has 4608 pixels horizontally and 3456 vertically.

When you multiply these 2 numbers, the result is about 16 million pixels, also written as 16 megapixels or 16M.

You can also determine the aspect ratio of the image from the Image Size setting. For example, the 4608 x 3456 setting yields an image 4 units wide for every 3 units tall, for a 4:3 aspect ratio. Most of the Image Size settings for the P1000 are in that ratio, which is a standard one for digital images, being the same shape as the camera's LCD. However, if you scroll down the lines of the Image Size menu, you will see a few entries that note a different aspect ratio.

Specifically, just below the setting for VGA (640 x 480), there is the entry for 4608 x 2592 pixels. At the far left on the line for this entry, above the number of megapixels, 12M, the menu shows the notation 16:9, meaning this Image Size setting is in a 16:9 aspect ratio: 16 units wide for every 9 units tall. This aspect ratio is another fairly common one, which corresponds to the shape of a widescreen HDTV set and is often called "widescreen."

On-screen 2 of the Image Size menu, another entry, 4608 x 3072, is labeled as 3:2, meaning its aspect ratio has 3 horizontal units for every 2 vertical ones. It is a common aspect ratio, which corresponds to the standard print size in the United States of 6 by 4 inches (15 by 10 cm).

Finally, the last entry on the Image size menu, 3456 x 3456 pixels, is in an aspect ratio of 1:1, resulting in a square image. Some photographers like to use this aspect ratio because of its symmetry or because it suits a particular composition.

With the Image Size menu setting, you have 2 choices to make. First, you can choose your images' resolution or number of pixels (megapixels). The larger the number of pixels, the larger you can make high-quality prints on paper, and the more options you have for cropping the image to highlight particular details from the exposure. Second, although most of the choices on the menu are in the standard 4:3 aspect ratio, you have the option of selecting an aspect ratio of 3:2, 16:9, or 1:1 if you want.

Of course, you can always just shoot with the maximum image size of 4608 x 3456 and then crop the image down in software later; in that way, you can use any aspect ratio you want, including those listed here or any other. But, if you want to use a 1:1 aspect ratio for creative reasons, or you want your landscape photo to have the 16:9 widescreen look. If you want to avoid being bothered with changing the aspect ratio in software, select an Image Size setting that corresponds to your desired aspect ratio so that the final result will come straight out of the camera. In addition, you will have the advantage of seeing how the final image will be composed as you set it up on the camera's display screen or in the viewfinder.

CHAPTER 3: TAKING GREAT PICTURES

Exploring Image Zone (Scene) Modes

The Coolpix P1000 has several scene modes. Scene modes are special settings designed to help you take good photos in different situations. Two scene modes are accessed through the mode dial: Bird-watching and Moon. There is also a general SCENE mode, accessed through the SCENE slot on the mode dial.

When you select the SCENE mode on the Coolpix P1000, you can choose from a list of 21 specific scene settings. These settings are designed to help you take better photos in different situations, such as Portrait, Landscape, Sports, Night Portrait, Party/Indoor, Beach, Snow, Sunset, Dusk/Dawn, Night Landscape, Close-up, Food, Fireworks Show, Backlighting, Easy Panorama, Pet Portrait, Soft, Selective Color, Multiple Exposure Lighten, Time-lapse Movie, and Superlapse Movie. The 22nd entry on the list is called Scene Auto Selector. This setting tells the camera to automatically choose the best scene mode for the scene you are shooting.

Scene modes differ from other shooting modes because they give the camera more control over the settings. When you select a scene mode, you tell the camera what photo you want to take (e.g., portrait, landscape, sports), and the camera will choose the best settings for the scene.

Other shooting modes, such as Aperture Priority and Shutter Priority, give you more control over the settings. In these

45

modes, you can choose the aperture or shutter speed, and the camera will adjust the other settings accordingly.

Some photographers prefer to avoid scene modes because they take away some control over the creative process. For example, when you're in scene mode, you can't set the white balance, metering mode, or ISO setting. You also can't use continuous shooting.

It means that the camera is making creative decisions for you. For example, the camera will choose the shutter speed and aperture for you. It can be frustrating for photographers who want more control over their photos.

Even though scene modes have some limitations, they can be helpful in certain situations. You don't have to use them for their labeled purposes only. For example, you might find that the Sports setting is suitable for taking photos of children playing, or the Sunset setting is suitable for taking photos of red flowers. The Bird-watching setting can also take photos of other types of wildlife, not just birds.

You need to know what each scene mode does before choosing the right one for your photo. Each scene mode changes various settings on the camera, such as the focus mode, flash status, shutter speed, and color sensitivity. I will discuss each scene mode in detail so you can make informed choices. I will start with the scene modes that have their slots on the mode dial, and then I will discuss the scene modes grouped under the SCENE setting. I will also include sample images for some of the most commonly used scene modes.

Moon

The Moon setting is on the mode dial next to the SCENE setting. It is indicated by a moon icon. The Coolpix P1000 has a long zoom lens, which makes it ideal for taking photos of the moon without having to use a telescope. The Moon setting automatically chooses the best settings for taking photos of the moon, such as the shutter speed, aperture, and ISO.

When you select the Moon setting, the camera will disable the flash and turn on the self-timer to 3 seconds. It is to prevent camera shake, which can blur your photos. You can change the self-timer to 10 seconds or turn it off. You can also use exposure compensation to make the moon appear brighter or darker in your photo. It is helpful if the moon is too bright or dim because of its phase. By default, the camera will focus on the center of the frame at infinity. It is the best setting for focusing on the moon. However, you can switch to manual focus if you prefer.

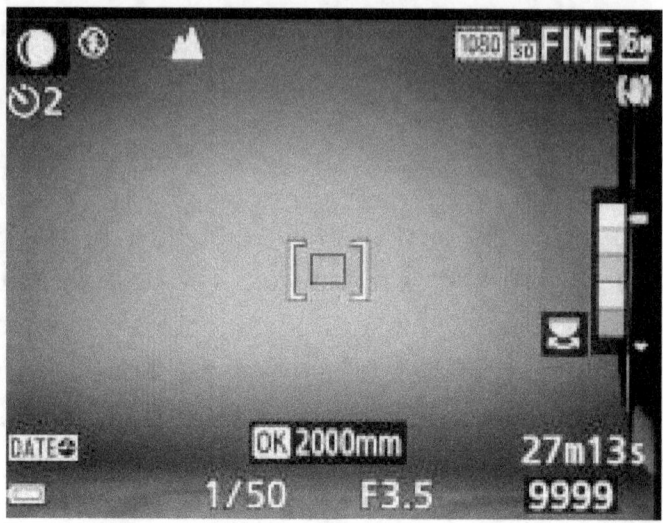

When you zoom the lens out to the widest setting, the camera will show you a small rectangle in the center of the screen. This rectangle represents the area of the scene that will be in focus when you zoom in to 1000mm. To center the moon in your photo, place the rectangle over the moon and press the OK button. The camera will zoom in to 1000mm, and the moon will be centered in the frame.

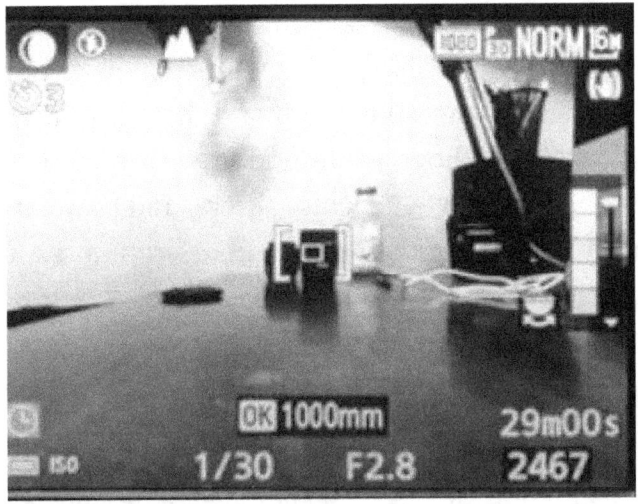

You can change the focal length of the small rectangle in Moon mode. To do this, go to the Shooting menu and select the Focal Length Selection option. You can choose from 1000mm, 2000mm, 2400mm, or 3000mm. The focal length you choose will be the focal length that the lens zooms to when you press the OK button in Moon mode.

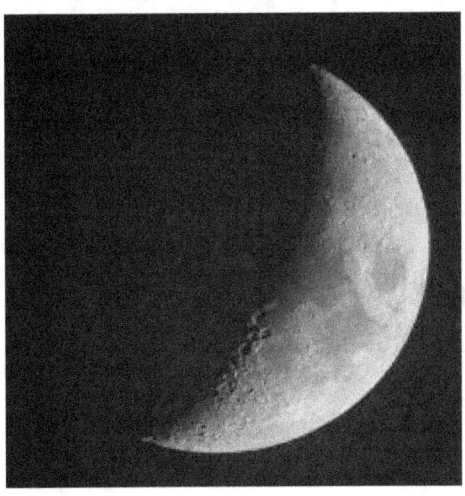

The camera also has a hue scale on the right side of the screen. This scale allows you to change the moon's color in your photos. To change the hue, turn the command dial. The top option is the default setting, showing the moon with no color change. The other options are virtual color filters, and they can be used to enhance your view of the moon and its craters. Try all of the different hue options to see which ones yield the best results for the type of image you are looking for.

Scene

The Bird-watching setting is designed to help you take better photos of birds. It is similar to the Moon setting, but it has a few additional features. For example, Bird-watching mode enables continuous shooting. It means that you can take a burst of photos with one shutter press. It is helpful for photographing birds in flight because it increases your chances of capturing a good image. To turn on continuous shooting, press the Menu button and select the Bird-watching menu. A bird icon at the top of the list of menu icons represents the Bird-watching menu.

To turn on continuous shooting in Bird-watching mode, press the OK or Right button to move to the next screen and select Continuous. Once continuous shooting is enabled, you can take a burst of photos by pressing and holding the shutter button. The camera will shoot about 7 photos per second.

When you are in Bird-watching mode, the camera will place a special frame in the center of the screen to indicate the area in view when you zoom in to 500mm. It is helpful for finding and centering a bird in your photo. To do this, start with a wide-angle view and place the bird in the small frame. Then, press the OK button, and the camera will automatically zoom in to 500mm. If you need to zoom back out to a wide-angle view, press the zoom lever to the left. If you want to zoom in further than 500mm, you can use the zoom lever to do that as well.

You can change the focal length of the special frame in Bird-watching mode. To do this, go to the Shooting menu and select the Focal Length Selection option. You can choose from 500mm, 800mm, 1000mm, 1400mm, 2000mm, or 3000mm. It helps frame your photo differently. For example, if you want to take a close-up photo of a bird's head, you would choose a higher focal length. In the photo you provided, the photographer used the Focal Length Selection option to choose a focal length of 3000mm. It allowed them to take a close-up photo of the bird's head.

The Scene Setting On The Mode Dial

When you switch the mode dial to SCENE on your camera, you can pick from 22 different options for settings, which include a general Scene Auto Selector and 21 specific scene types like landscapes or portraits.

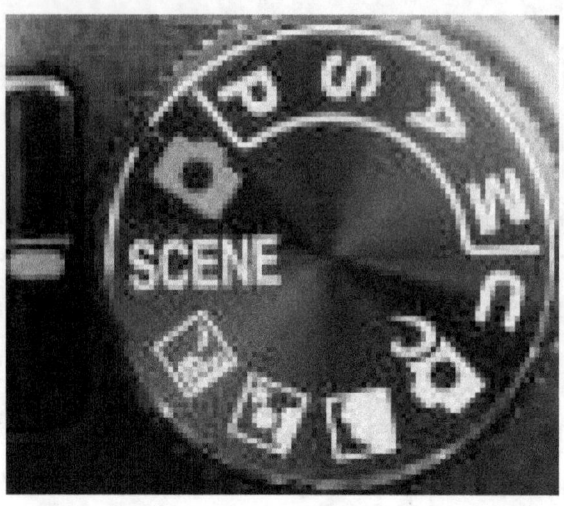

To choose one of these options, press the Menu button and pick a scene type from the menu that shows up on the screen. You can move through these options using the multi-selector dial or the Up and Down buttons on your camera.

When you select any of the 22 Scene mode settings, the menu offers few other choices; that is, when you select such as sunset from the Scene menu, you cannot make any other choices except Image Size and Image Quality. The camera will make other settings as it deems appropriate for that selection. These Scene mode settings are convenient if you are faced with a certain type of photographic situation and you want the camera to make reasonable choices for that situation. Still, you have little control over the camera's other settings. Following are details about each of the types. I will include sample images for several of the selections.

Scene Auto Selector

In the first choice, the camera looks at the scene and tries to figure out which shooting mode is best. It can pick from options like Portrait, Landscape, Night Portrait, Night Landscape, Close-up, Backlighting, and Other Shooting Conditions. If the camera thinks the scene matches one of these settings, it shows a little picture of that setting in the upper left corner of the screen.

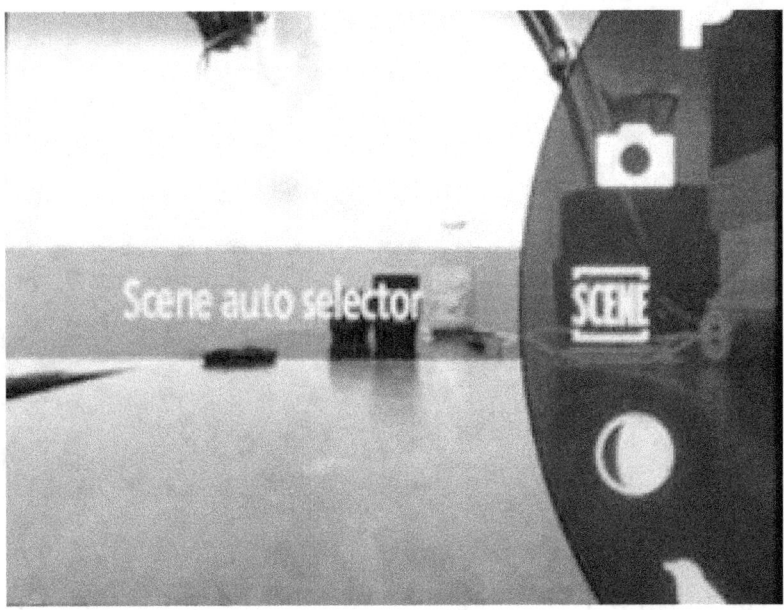

When using Portrait or Night Portrait, if the camera sees more than two subjects, it shows a slightly different icon with the number 1. In Portrait mode, the camera makes the skin look smoother when it detects faces, which is the same for Night Portrait mode. In Backlighting mode, it shows an icon with the number 1 if it finds human subjects instead of non-human things.

In Scene Auto Selector mode on your camera, you can adjust things like exposure and use a self-timer, but you can't pick the way the camera focuses or choose how the flash works. The camera will suggest using the flash and set it to Auto mode, meaning the camera decides when to use the flash.

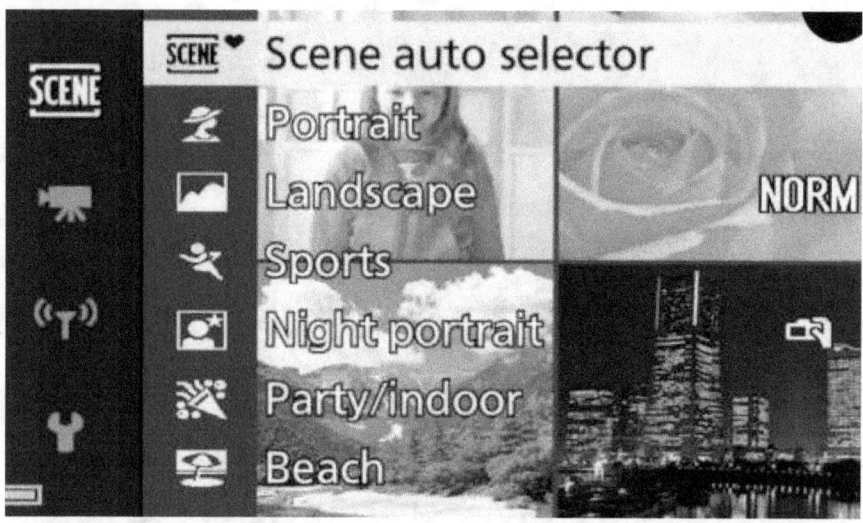

If the camera picks a scene mode you don't like, you can always switch to a different mode like Auto, Program, or a specific Scene mode setting using the mode dial.

After the Scene Auto Selector option, there are 21 specific settings. In these settings, you can only change Image Quality and Image Size, which you'll find at the bottom of the list of scene types on the menu.

But, there are certain settings like Night Portrait, Night Landscape, Close-up, Backlighting, Easy Panorama, Pet Portrait, Multiple Exposure Lighten, Time-lapse Movie, and Superlapse Movie. These settings have special menus with choices you can make, such as using your hand or a tripod, taking one picture or multiple in a row, and other options. I'll explain more about these 21 settings and their choices in the following section.

Portrait

In the Portrait setting, the camera does a few things automatically. It looks for human faces and focuses on the one closest to the camera. It also makes the skin on faces look smoother. You can choose the flash and pick the flash mode you want. You can't change how the camera focuses (though you can choose manual focus if you want). You can use the self-timer or smile timer and adjust the exposure.

Landscape

I often use the Landscape setting on my camera to capture scenes of landscapes, buildings, and similar things. When you choose this setting from the menu, you'll see the Landscape option, which gives you two choices: Noise Reduction Burst or Single Shot.

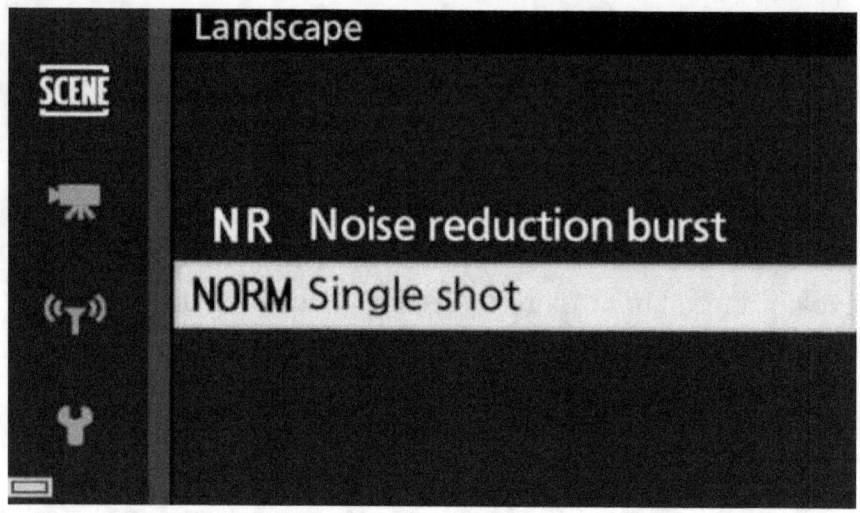

If you pick Noise Reduction Burst, the camera takes many quick pictures using a higher ISO setting and combines them into one image inside the camera. It helps reduce the grainy or speckled look when using high ISO settings. But, because of this process, the final picture will be a bit cropped, meaning you won't capture the entire scene. This setting is handy when taking photos in low light to lessen the unwanted grainy look from a high ISO setting.

If you choose the Single Shot option, the camera acts like a regular Landscape mode. It takes only one picture with a lower ISO setting, which usually makes the picture sharper compared to the Noise Reduction Burst mode.

Sports
The Sports setting on your camera is for capturing things that move quickly. When you press and hold the shutter button, the camera takes a bunch of pictures in a row, up to seven shots per

second, depending on the situation. The flash won't pop up, and the focus and exposure stay the same after the first picture to make the photos happen faster. You can adjust the exposure, but you can't use the self-timer. This mode is handy when you want to freeze action in well-lit places.

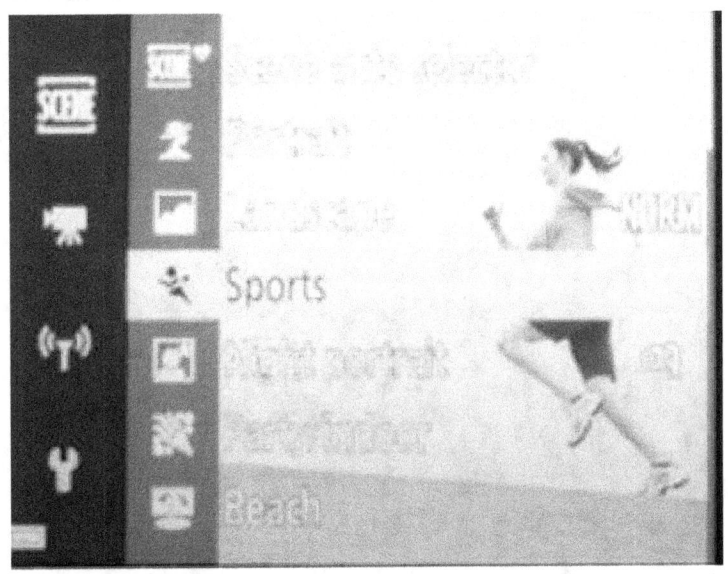

The Sports setting is suitable for capturing fast-moving action with a quick series of shots. But, it has a limitation. After taking rapid shots, the camera needs time to save those pictures to the memory card. If you want to take another great shot immediately, you'll have to wait until the camera finishes saving the previous pictures.

Keep this limitation in mind and prepare for it. If you need to take more fast shots within about five seconds after the first set, switch to a different setting like Program mode. Use single shooting or, if needed, a slower burst mode that takes only a couple of shots. This way, your camera will be ready for more action faster.

Night Portrait

The Night Portrait scene mode on the Coolpix P1000 is designed to help you take better portraits of people in low light conditions. It does this by using a slow shutter speed to capture more light, and by boosting the contrast and saturation of the skin tones. This can help to create more flattering and natural-looking portraits.

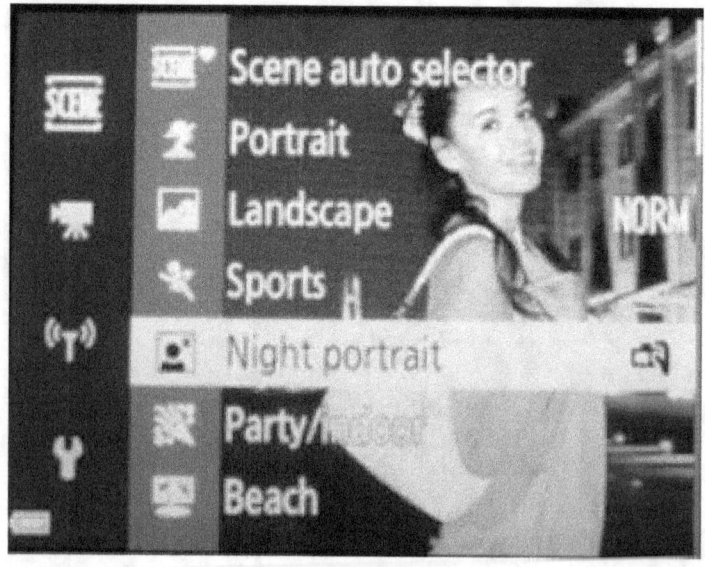

Party/Indoor

This setting is designed for taking pictures indoors, like of people and rooms. In most cases, it's a good idea to use the flash. The flash mode is initially set to Auto with Red-eye Reduction, but you can change it to another flash mode if you prefer. If you don't want to use the flash, keep it down, and the camera will use a slower shutter speed. In this case, it's essential to hold the camera very steady or place it on a tripod, but realistically, you might not use it for spontaneous photos at a party. The camera will focus on the subject in the middle of the frame.

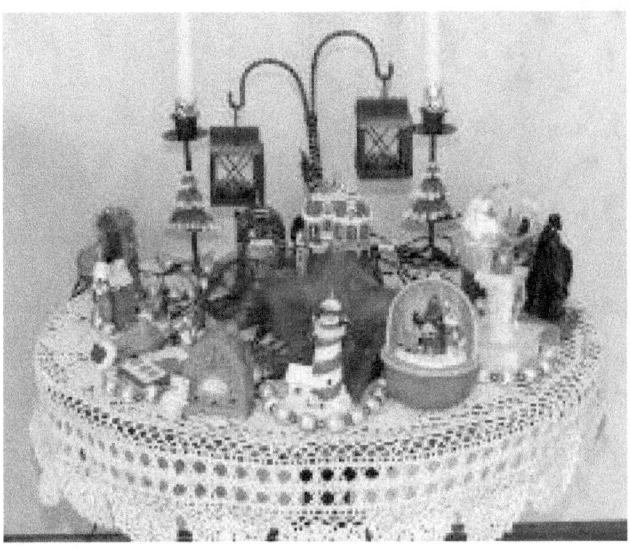

I used the flash to take a picture, and the camera automatically chose a shutter speed of 1/13 second, an aperture of f/4.2, and an ISO of 800. When using the Party/Indoor setting, you can adjust the exposure or use the self-timer, but you can't change how the camera focuses.

Beach

When you choose the Beach setting, the camera adjusts its settings for bright sunlight typically found at the beach. In such conditions, the camera might make the main subject appear too dark because it's measuring the brightness of the beach.

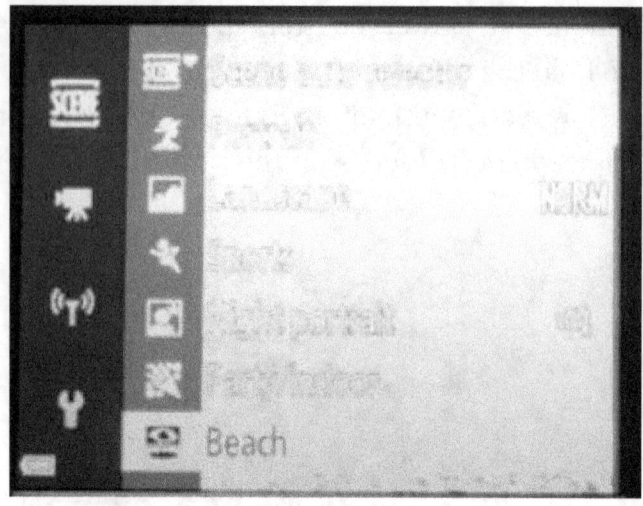

If you raise the flash, the camera will set it to Auto mode to properly light up the subject. It usually makes the flash go off so the subject looks clear against the bright background. You can change the flash mode if you want. But it's not necessary to use the flash with the Beach setting.

You can pick between macro focus for close-up shots or regular autofocus for normal shots, but you can't manually focus or use infinity focus. You can also use the self-timer or adjust the exposure.

Snow

The Snow scene mode on the Coolpix P1000 is designed to help you take better photos of snow scenes. It does this by boosting the contrast and saturation of the colors, and by reducing the blue cast that can sometimes appear in snow photos. This can help to create more vibrant and realistic-looking photos.

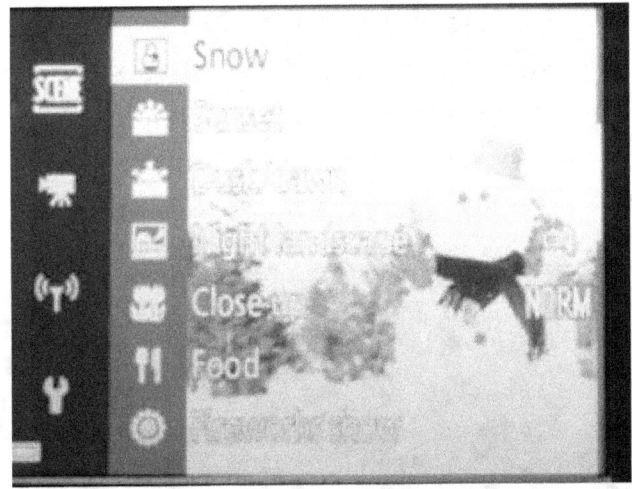

Sunset

In this setting, the camera turns off the flash, but you can still use the self-timer and adjust the exposure. You can't change the focus mode; it stays on infinity autofocus.

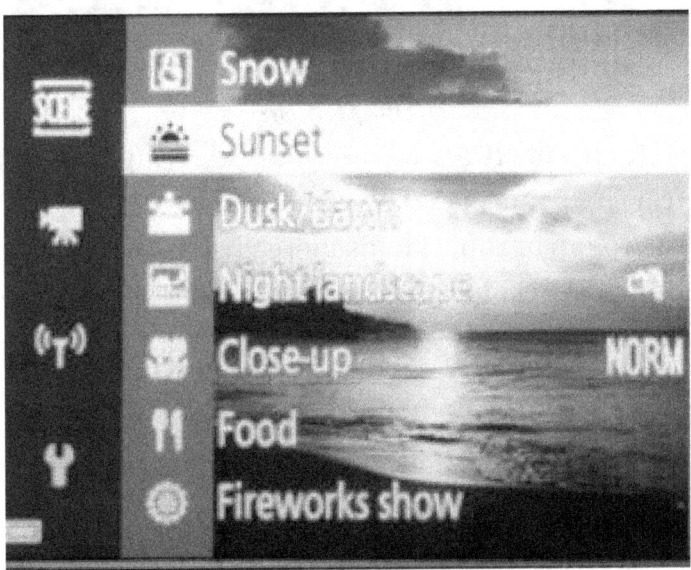

The camera enhances the red tones in the late afternoon or early morning sunlight when you take a shot. You don't have to use this setting only for what it's labeled. For instance, if you're capturing autumn leaves or red-brick buildings and you want to make the red colors stand out more, this setting can help.

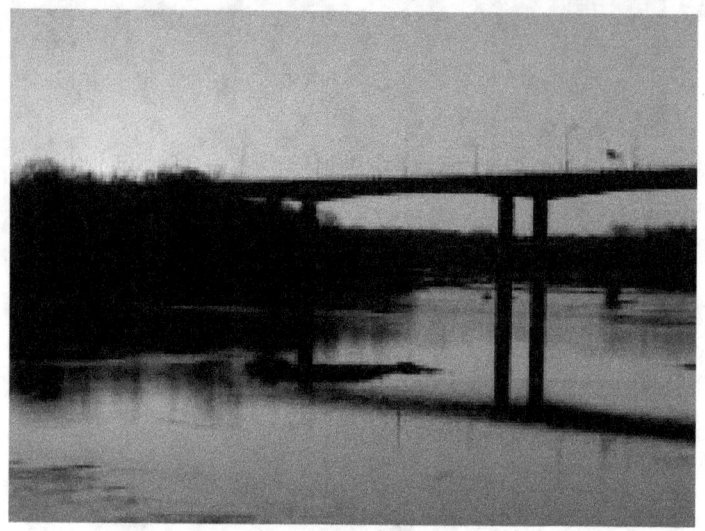

Dusk/Dawn

If you're taking pictures before sunrise or after sunset, this setting can be beneficial. The camera turns off the flash and makes the colors in your photos more vivid to make them more interesting. It's great for when the light is dim and your pictures might otherwise look dull or faded.

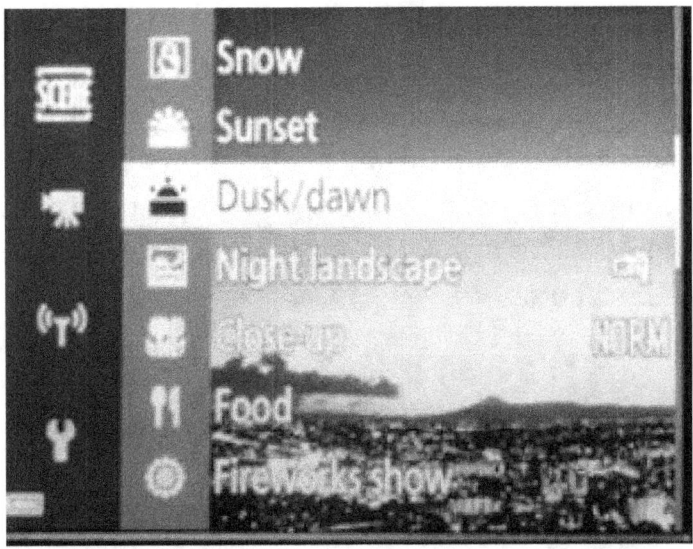

You can't change most camera settings in this mode, but you can adjust the exposure and use the self-timer. This setting highlights the purplish or bluish tones you often see during twilight or early mornings.

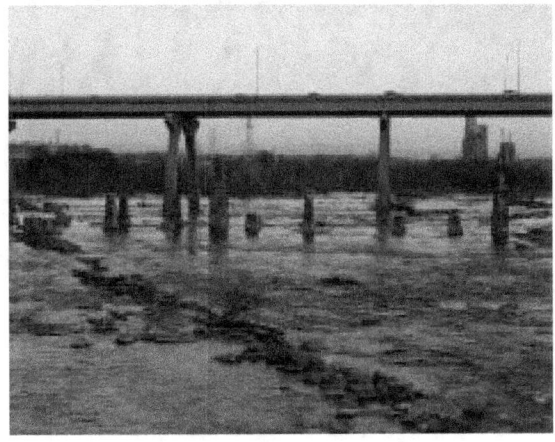

Night Landscape

The Night Landscape scene mode on the Coolpix P1000 is designed to help you take better photos of landscapes in low light conditions. It does this by using a slow shutter speed to capture more light, and by boosting the contrast and saturation of the colors. This can help to create more dramatic and atmospheric photos.

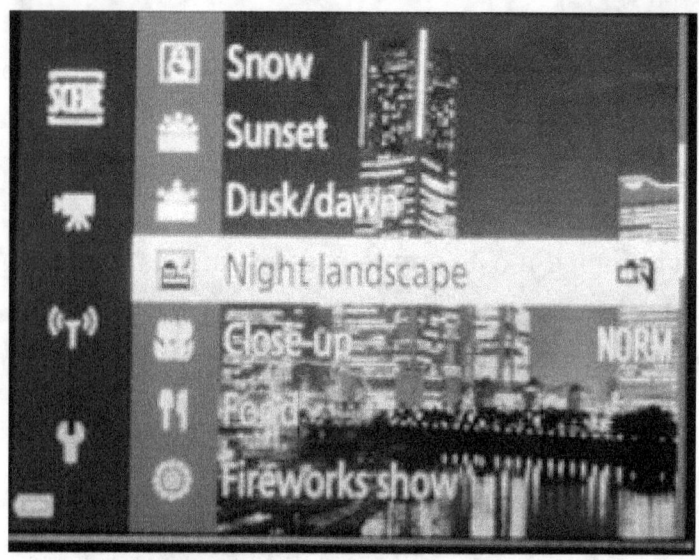

To use the Night Landscape scene mode, simply select it from the mode dial on the top of the camera. Then, point the camera at the scene you want to photograph and press the shutter button. The camera will automatically choose the best settings for the scene.

Close-up

With this setting, the camera goes into a special mode for taking pictures of things that are close. If you zoom in with the lens, the camera will automatically zoom back out to get the subject in focus (but you can zoom back in if you prefer). You can use the self-timer or adjust the exposure, but you can't change the focus mode; it stays on macro.

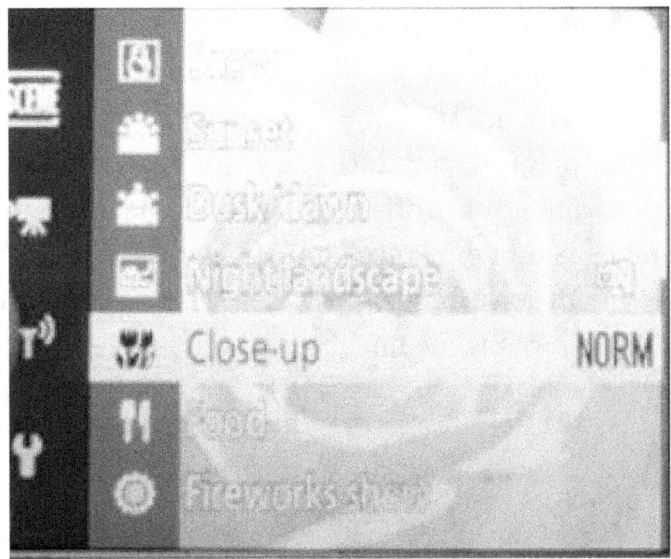

The camera also sets the AF Area Mode to Manual (Spot). It means you can decide exactly where the camera should focus. To do this, press the OK button in the middle of the buttons on the camera, and then use the direction buttons to move the focus area around the screen to where you want it to focus. You can also use the buttons to move the frame around the screen. It will move up and down or side to side.

If you need to use one of the direction buttons for something else, like setting a timer, using the flash, or adjusting the exposure, press the OK button again, and those functions will be available. Press the OK button again if you need to move the focus area again. In this mode, the camera continuously adjusts the focus until you press the shutter button halfway down to lock in the focus.

Like some other scene modes, the Close-up setting allows you to pick between Noise Reduction Burst or Single Shot in the Scene menu. You can choose one of these options by selecting Close-up in the menu. With Noise Reduction Burst, the camera quickly takes pictures to reduce the graininess caused by high ISO settings, and it turns off the flash. In Single Shot mode, the camera takes just one picture and lets you raise the flash and pick the type of flash mode you want. The camera also adds contrast and sharpens the image's edges in Single Shot mode.

You can use a different shooting mode like Program or Auto and manually choose macro focus by pressing the focus button (usually the Down button). However, if you want to set up the camera quickly for close-up shots, it's handy to have this scene setting ready. To get sharp close-up pictures, it's essential to keep the camera still to prevent blurriness. Using a tripod or monopod is the best way, but that's only sometimes practical in real-life situations.

Food

This setting is similar to the Close-up setting discussed above, though it does not offer Noise Reduction Burst mode; only single shots are available. The camera switches to macro focus mode and zooms back if necessary to focus on a nearby subject. It turns off the flash and switches to a slightly higher ISO setting in Food scene mode. It is to avoid using the flash, which can wash out the colors of food and make it look less appealing. The higher ISO setting helps ensure the photo is properly exposed, even in low light conditions.

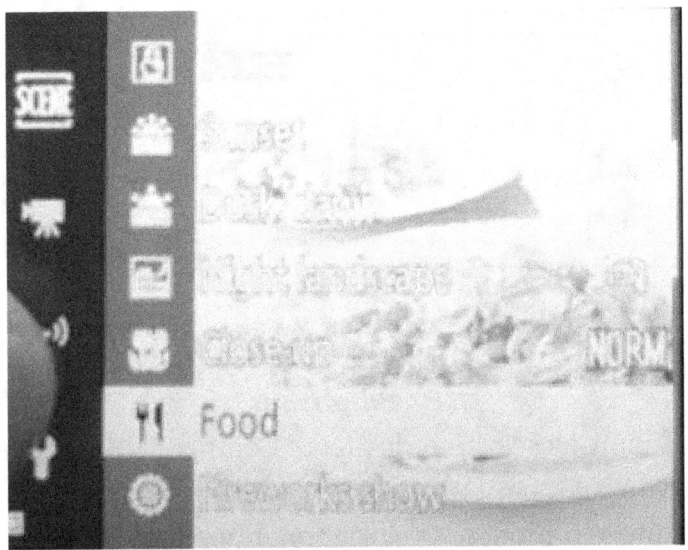

Fireworks Show

The Fireworks Show scene mode on the Coolpix P1000 is designed to help you take better photos of fireworks displays. It does this by using a slow shutter speed to capture more light from the fireworks and by automatically adjusting the ISO and aperture settings to ensure that your photos are properly exposed.

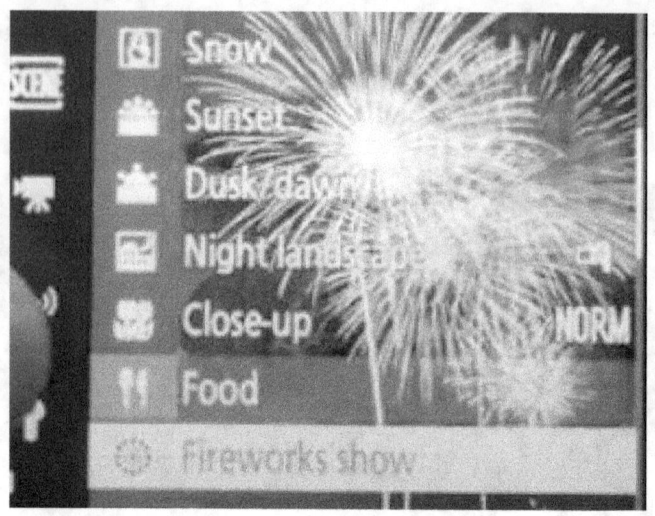

Backlighting

The Backlighting scene mode on the Coolpix P1000 is designed to help you take better photos of backlit subjects. It can be a challenging situation, as the bright light behind the subject can make it appear dark and underexposed.

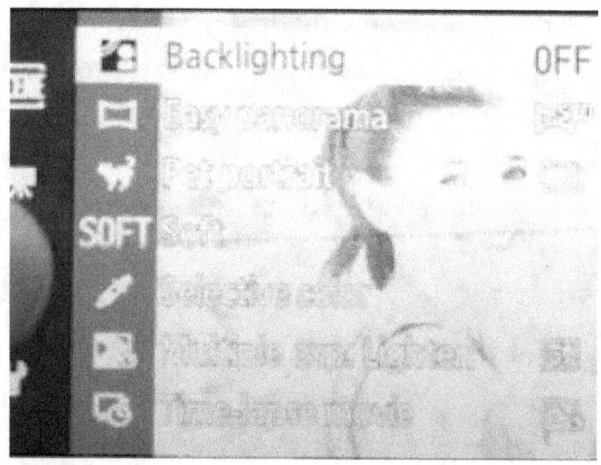

The Backlighting scene mode works by automatically adjusting the camera's exposure settings to ensure that both the subject and the background are properly exposed. It also uses a technique called fill-flash to reduce shadows and highlights.

To use the Backlighting scene mode, select it from the mode dial on the top of the camera. Then, point the camera at the subject you want to photograph and press the shutter button. The camera will automatically choose the best settings for the scene.

Easy Panorama

The Easy Panorama scene mode on the Coolpix P1000 is a great way to take panoramic photos without stitching them together later. This mode works by automatically taking a series of photos and then stitching them together to create a single panoramic image.

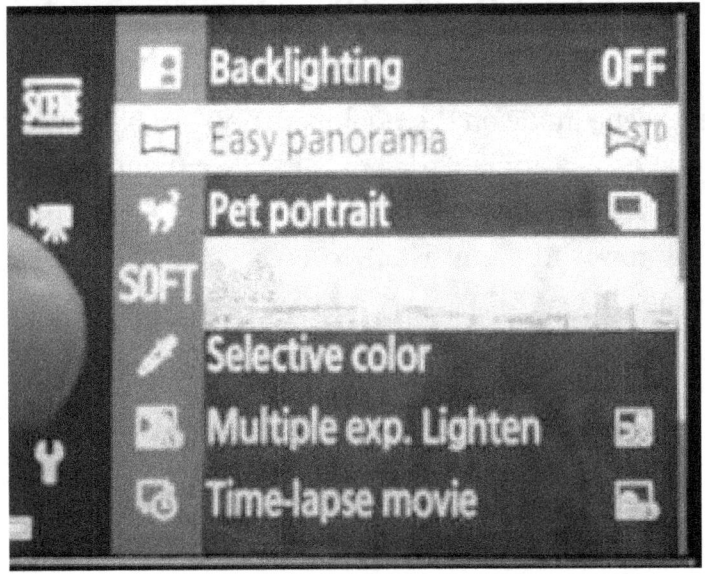

Pet Portrait

The Pet Portrait scene mode on the Coolpix P1000 is designed to help you take better photos of your pets. It does this by automatically adjusting the camera's settings to ensure that your pet is focused and that the background is blurred. It helps to create a more flattering and professional-looking photo of your pet.

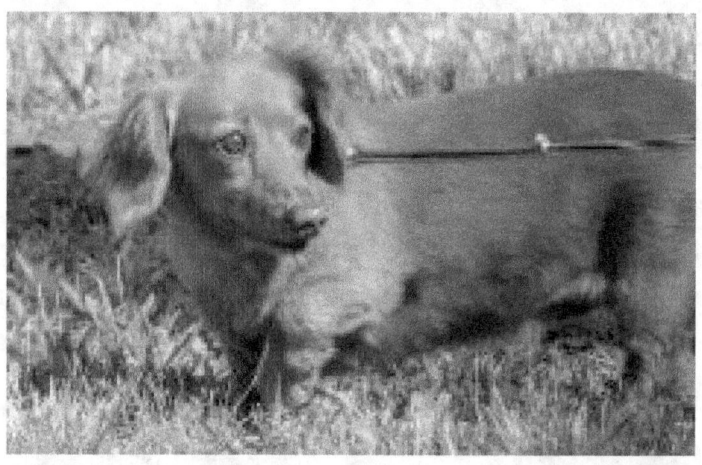

Soft

The Soft scene mode on the Coolpix P1000 is a post-processing effect that can be applied to photos to make them appear softer and more diffused. It can be a helpful effect for portraits and other photos where you want to create a more flattering or artistic look.

Selective Color

The Selective Color scene mode on the Coolpix P1000 allows you to create photos where only certain colors are displayed in color, while the rest of the photo is in black and white. It can be a creative way to emphasize certain elements in your photo and create a more eye-catching image. When using the Selective Color scene mode, select it from the mode dial on the top of the camera. Then, point the camera at the scene you want to photograph and press the shutter button. The camera will automatically choose the best settings for the scene.

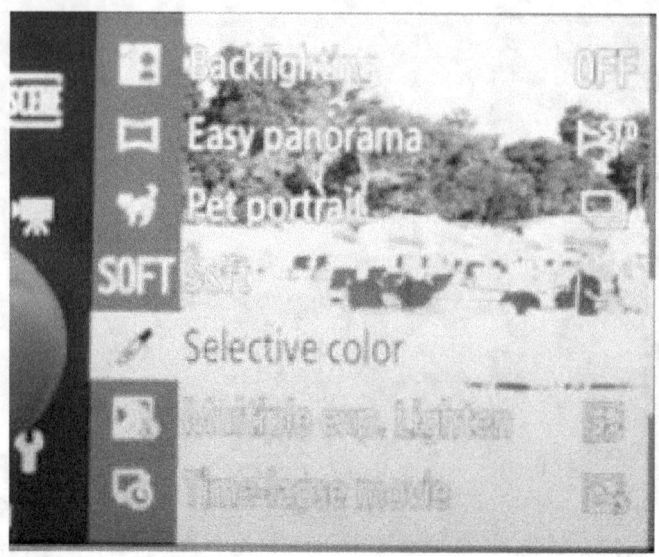

You can also use the multi-selector to highlight a specific color in the scene. To do this:

1. Press the A (AE-L/AF-L) button to lock the focus and exposure.
2. Press the multi-selector to move the cursor over the color you want to highlight.
3. Press the A (AE-L/AF-L) button again to lock the selection. The camera will then display a photo preview with the selected color highlighted in color.

You can adjust the size and position of the selection using the multi-selector. When satisfied with the selection, press the OK button to take the photo.

Multiple Exposure Lighten

The Multiple Exposure Lighten scene mode on the Coolpix P1000 allows you to take multiple photos and then combine them into a single image, with the lightest pixels from each image being used to create the final image. It can be a helpful technique for creating photos with a high dynamic range (HDR) or a more ethereal or dreamy look.

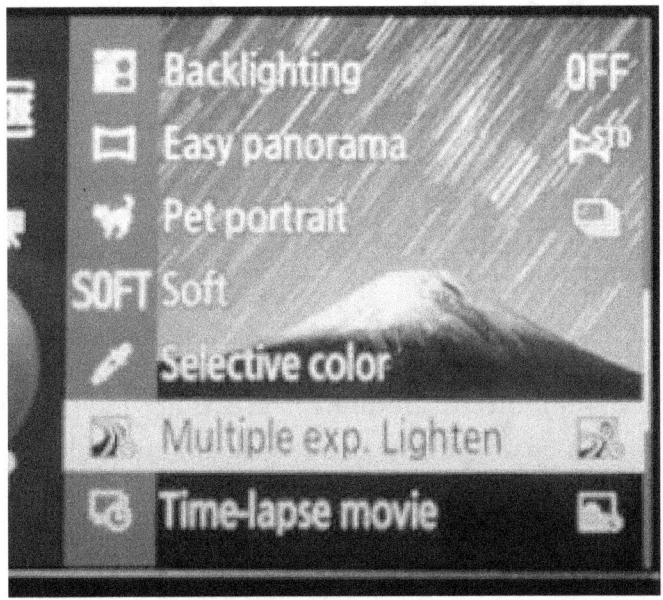

Time-lapse Movie

The Time-Lapse Movie scene mode on the Coolpix P1000 allows you to create time-lapse movies. Time-lapse movies are created by taking photos at a set interval and then stitching them into a single video.

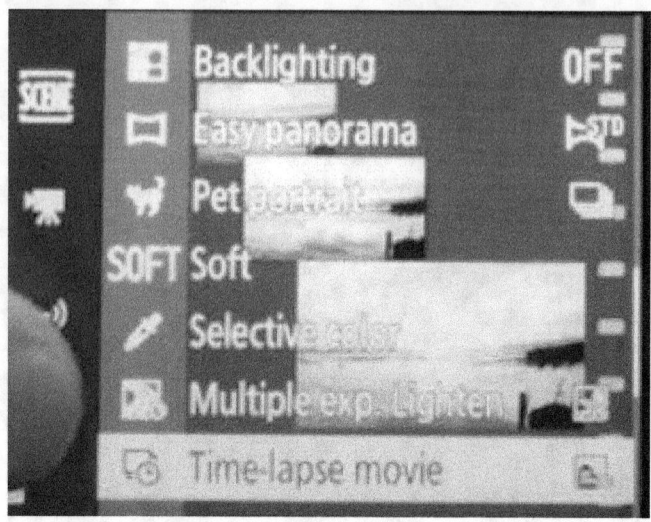

It can be a valuable technique for creating videos of natural phenomena, such as sunsets or the movement of clouds. It can also be used to create videos of events that take place over a long period, such as the construction of a building or the growth of a plant.

Superlapse Movie

The Superlapse Movie mode on the Coolpix P1000 is a special mode that allows you to create time-lapse movies of moving subjects. This mode is similar to the Time-Lapse Movie mode, but it uses a faster shutter speed to freeze the subject's motion. It is useful for creating time-lapse movies of sports events, wildlife, or other fast-moving subjects.

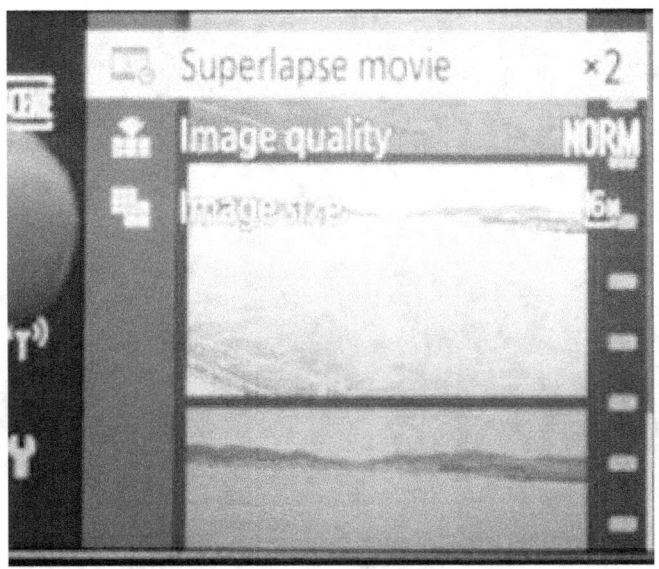

Focus

To change the focus mode, press the down button (marked with a flower icon). It will open a small menu with three options: AF (normal autofocus), the flower icon (macro/closeup focus), and the mountain icon (infinity focus). Use the directional buttons to select the top icon, AF (normal autofocus), and press OK to confirm your choice. The letters AF will appear in the upper left corner of the display for a few seconds and then disappear because that is the default setting.

Next, press the Menu button on the back of the camera to open the shooting menu. Scroll through the menu items with the up and down buttons until the yellow highlight is on the line for AF Area Mode on the second screen. Press OK to select the item, then use the up and down buttons to select Manual (Normal).

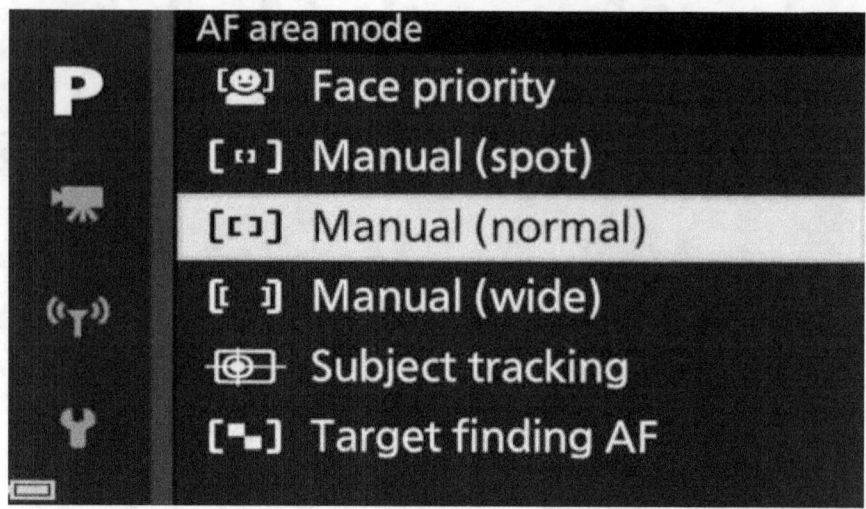

Press OK to confirm your selection, then half-press the shutter button to go to the shooting screen. You should see a focus frame with four arrows. If you don't see the arrows, press OK to make them appear.

In Manual (Normal) mode, the camera will place a focus frame in the center of the screen. You can move the frame around the screen with the directional buttons or the multi-selector dial. Press OK to confirm, and the focus frame will be locked in its current position. Aiming the camera, center your subject between the white focus brackets.

Half-press the shutter button to let the camera evaluate exposure and focus. You'll hear a beep, and the focus brackets will turn green to confirm focus.

If you're happy with how everything looks, press the shutter button down to take the picture.

To take a picture with the main subject off-center, place the focus frame over the subject and half-press the shutter button to focus and lock in focus and exposure. Then, move the camera to create the desired composition, with the subject at the right. Finally, press the shutter button to take the picture, and the area you originally focused on will be in focus.

Manual Focus

Manual focus is another popular option among photographers, who appreciate the control it offers. In some situations, such as low light, glass or wire fences, extreme close-ups, or multiple objects at different distances, manual focus may be the best option for ensuring that the desired subject is in sharp focus.

To use manual focus, turn the focus mode selector to MF. When you first switch to manual focus, the screen will be displayed at its normal magnification or two or four times its normal magnification.

Nikon's magnification options can be confusing, so here's a brief explanation. Figure 2-10 shows the shooting screen in manual focus mode. The icons below the shutter speed and aperture values indicate which buttons to press to change the magnification.

In this example, the x4 indicator is next to the Left button, meaning you can press the Left button to change the magnification to four times normal. The AF letters are next to the Right button, meaning you can press the Right button to use autofocus. The x1 indicator is next to the Down button, meaning you can press the Down button to return the image to normal size.

I find this notation confusing because it doesn't show the current magnification. You have to decode it based on the available options. To decode it, look at the leftmost position. If you see a 4, the magnification is 2x, and you can press the Left button to switch to 4x.

If you see a 2, the magnification is 1x, and you can press the Left button to switch to 2x. If you see a 1, the magnification is 4x, and you can press the Left button to switch to 1x. The magnification used in manual focus is saved from the last time manual focus was used, so it will vary depending on your previous setting.

Once in manual focus mode, turn the multi-selector dial to adjust focus. Watch the focus scale on the right side of the screen and turn the dial until the focus is as sharp as possible. You can press the Left button to change the magnification or the Down button to lock focus and return to normal size (x1 on the display). After returning to normal size, press the Down button to magnify the screen and resume adjusting focus.

As you turn the multi-selector dial, a white bar will move up and down on the focus scale. (The bar turns green when the focus is in the macro range.) Adjust until the focus is as sharp as possible, then take the picture.

To switch to another function, such as adjusting the aperture in Aperture Priority mode, press the Down button to lock focus and return the screen to normal size. Then, use the dial for the other function. To return to manual focus, press the Down button again.

To use autofocus, press the Right button as prompted on the display. The camera will autofocus on the subject in the center of the screen. You can then adjust the focus manually using the multi-selector dial. To manually focus on the control ring, turn it until the focus is sharp. You can also use the side zoom control for manual focus if it's assigned to that function in the Setup menu.

If you have Peaking turned on in the Setup menu, you can turn the command dial to adjust the intensity of the Peaking effect on the scale from 0 to 5 at the left of the display. This feature displays more white pixels in the areas of sharp focus as the focus gets sharper.

CHAPTER 4: TAKING CHARGE OF EXPOSURE

Exposure Compensation

The camera has an exposure compensation control allows you to adjust the exposure in unusual or non-optimal lighting conditions.

For example, the camera's autoexposure system may underexpose a dark green model car in front of a white background since the large expanse of white will make the camera think that the scene is brighter than it is.

To solve this problem, you can use the exposure compensation control. This control is labeled with plus and minus signs, with the plus on a black background and the minus on white. Pressing the right button on the multi-selector activates the exposure compensation system, which allows you to override the automatic exposure by up to ±3 EV.

Set the camera to Program mode and aim at your subject. You can also use Auto mode, as exposure compensation is available in both modes. Press the Right button on the multi-selector to display a vertical scale on the right side of the display, with a plus sign at the top and a minus sign at the bottom.

To adjust the exposure compensation, press the Up and Down buttons, turn the multi-selector dial, or rotate the command dial. The yellow tick marks on the scale indicate the current exposure compensation value. Moving the tick marks to the bottom of the scale will make the image significantly darker than the automatic exposure. Moving the tick marks to the top will make the image noticeably brighter.

The camera screen previews the exposure changes as you adjust the exposure compensation. The camera also displays a histogram on the left side of the screen, a chart showing the distribution of brightness values in the image. In this case, you would increase the exposure compensation to brighten the image so that the model car is properly exposed and the background is a brighter white.

After taking the picture, reset the exposure compensation to zero in the middle of the scale to avoid unintentionally affecting future photos. The camera retains the exposure compensation value you set, even when turned off and on again. If a positive or negative exposure compensation value is set, the camera displays the value and exposure compensation icon in the lower right corner of the display.

White Balance

One challenge in photography is that film and digital camera sensors do not respond to colors in the same way that the human eye does. When we look at a scene in daylight or indoors under various artificial lighting, we do not generally notice a difference in the hues of the objects we see, regardless of the light source. However, cameras cannot correct for color temperature automatically. The camera "sees" colors differently depending on the color temperature of the light that illuminates the subject or scene.

81

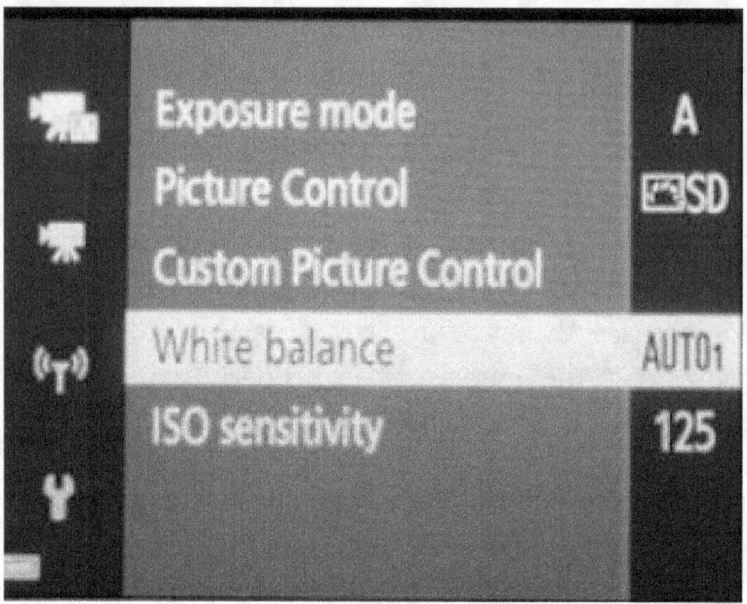

Color temperature is a measure of the warmth or coolness of light, expressed in kelvins (K). A lower kelvin rating indicates a warmer, more reddish light, while a higher kelvin rating indicates a cooler, more bluish light. For example, candlelight has a color temperature of about 1,800 K, indoor tungsten light has a color temperature of about 3,000 K, outdoor sunlight and electronic flash have a color temperature of about 5,500 K, and outdoor shade has a color temperature of about 7,000 K.

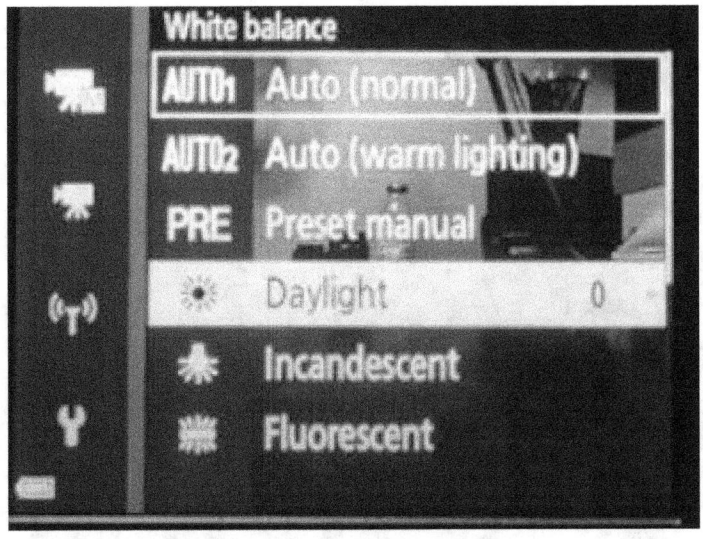

If you are using a film camera, you may need to use a colored filter in front of the lens or light source to correct the color temperature of the light source. Color film is rated to reproduce colors accurately at a particular color temperature. For example, film rated for daylight use will produce accurate colors when used outdoors in daylight. However, if you use the same film indoors, the resulting image will have a reddish cast because the color temperature of indoor lighting is lower than that of daylight. To correct this, you can use a color filter that warms the light to match the color temperature of the film.

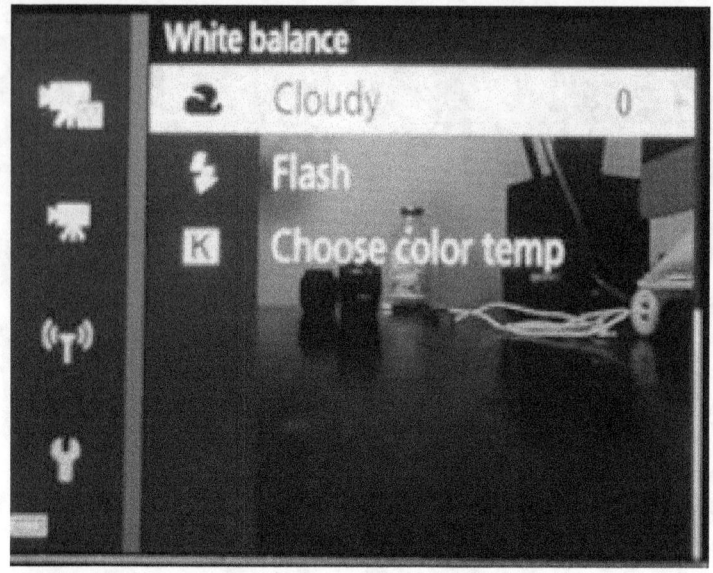

Modern digital cameras can adjust their electronic circuitry to correct the white balance, which is the term for balancing the color temperature of an image. The Nikon Coolpix P1000, like most digital cameras, has a White Balance setting that allows you to choose the proper color correction for any given light source. To access this setting, press the Menu button and navigate the Shooting menu.

Once you've selected the White Balance option, which is the fifth one on the first screen of the Shooting menu, press either the OK button or the Right button. It will display a list of White Balance choices, each represented by an icon, word, or abbreviation. The options include Auto (normal), Auto (warm lighting), Preset Manual, Daylight, Incandescent, Fluorescent, Cloudy, Flash, and Choose Color Temperature.

The white balance settings are self-explanatory. To select a setting, press the Up or Down button to highlight it and press the OK button to confirm. If you select Auto, you are done. There are no further adjustments available. If you select one of the other settings, you can fine-tune it using the Up and Down buttons.

If you select Daylight, Incandescent, Cloudy, or Flash, you can press the Right button to open a screen with a scale on the left from -3 to +3. Use the Up and Down buttons or the multi-selector dial to move the yellow selection block up and down the scale to select a value. A positive value will bias the white balance towards a bluish tint, while a negative value will bias it towards a reddish tint.

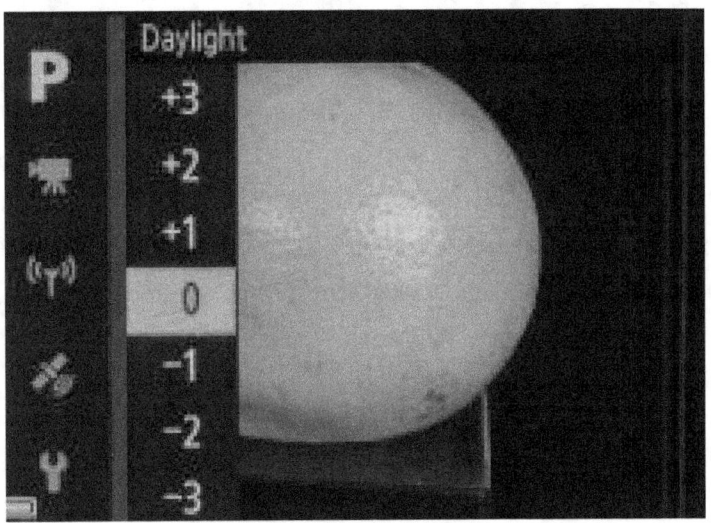

If you select Fluorescent, pressing the Right button opens a screen with three choices: 1, 2, and 3—these three sub-varieties of fluorescent light range from white to neutral to daylight. There are no other adjustments available with this setting.

Suppose you use a white balance setting with an adjustment scale (Daylight, Incandescent, Fluorescent, Cloudy, or Flash). In that case, you must press the OK button to confirm the setting after selecting an adjustment amount, even if it is zero. The new white balance setting will not take effect until you do.

Finally, you can manually set the white balance by selecting Preset Manual. This option is useful when dealing with mixed light sources or a reddish or unusual light source. To do this, highlight the Preset Manual and press the OK button or the Right button. The next screen will allow you to cancel or measure the white balance.

Highlight Measure and aim the square in the center of the screen at a white or gray surface illuminated by the light source you will use. Then, press the OK button. The camera will measure the white balance and store the setting. To use this setting now or in the future, select Preset Manual, even after the camera has been turned off and on again.

You can use the Preset Manual setting to add a creative color tint to your scenes. For example, you can set the white balance manually using a red or orange surface, which will give your photos a pronounced blue tint. Just reset the white balance to Auto or another normal setting when you're done.

The last option on the second screen of the White Balance menu is Choose Color Temperature. Highlight this option and press the OK or Right button to open a screen with a scale of 2500 K to 10,000 K on the left.

You can use this scale to set the white balance for a specific color temperature if you know it. You can determine the color temperature of a light source using a color temperature meter.

A color temperature meter is a good option for precise white balance settings, but it is expensive. If you don't have a meter, you can still use the Choose Color Temperature option, but you must guess or use your sense of color. For example, if you are shooting under incandescent light, you can start with a setting of 3,000 K and then adjust the value until the colors look natural on the camera's display. Lowering the color temperature setting will make the image cooler (bluish) while raising the setting will make the image warmer (more reddish). Once you find the best setting, leave it in place and start shooting.

Auto 1, Preset Manual, Daylight, Fluorescent 2, Flash, and Choose Color Temperature (using a value of 5000) all produced good color balance. Auto 2, Fluorescent 3, and Cloudy would be acceptable, but the results could be improved with further adjustments to tweak the bluish or reddish tint. The only settings that I would not recommend using in this situation are Incandescent and Fluorescent 1. In general, I leave the White Balance set to Auto 1, but it is helpful to know that I can make more customized settings when needed.

ISO Sensitivity

ISO measures a photographic film or digital sensor's sensitivity to light. A higher ISO rating means the film or sensor is more light-sensitive. Therefore, when shooting an image or video with a high ISO value, you need less light to achieve a normal exposure than you would with a lower value. It allows you to use a faster shutter speed, narrower aperture, or both than you could with a lower ISO.

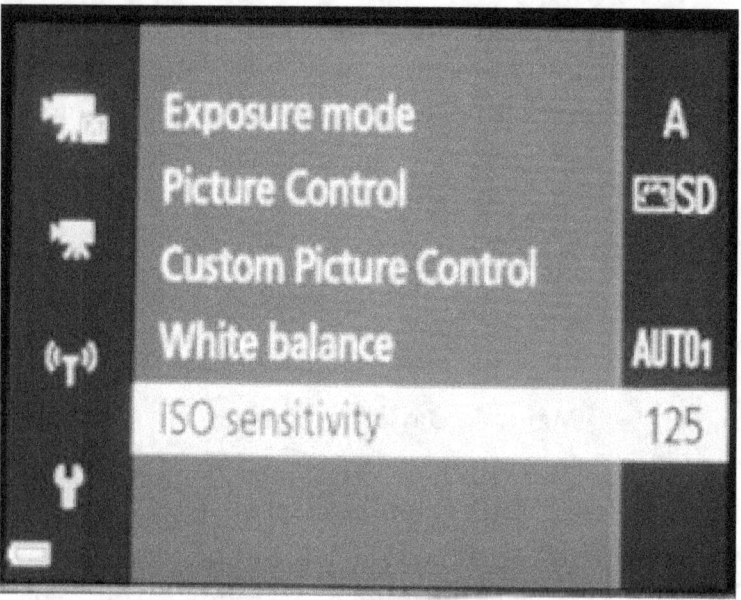

The downside of using higher ISO values is that the sensor is more likely to produce visual noise, which makes the image appear grainy. Camera manufacturers have significantly progressed in developing sensors that can use high ISO values without too much noise. However, there is still some loss of quality, especially at the highest ISO values.

Generally, shoot images with the lowest ISO possible to achieve proper exposure. An exception is if you want the grainy look of high ISO for creative purposes. For example, indoors in low light, you may set the ISO to 800 to expose the image with a reasonably fast shutter speed. Otherwise, a slow shutter speed could cause a blurry image.

To summarize: Shoot with low ISO settings (usually 100 on the P900) whenever possible. Use high ISO settings (400 or higher, up to 1600 or even 3200 or 6400) when necessary to use a fast shutter speed to freeze the action and avoid blur or when desired to achieve a creative grainy effect.

To set the ISO on the Nikon P900, press the Menu button and navigate to the ISO Sensitivity line on the second screen of the Shooting menu. Press the Right button to open the ISO setting screen.

CHAPTER 5: CAPTURING VIDEO

Capturing Still Images While Recording Movies

You can take a still photo while recording a video without interrupting the recording! Just press the shutter button all the way down. The camera will save the photo as a JPEG image and keep recording the video.

You can only take still photos while the camera icon is displayed on the screen. If you see the camera off icon, you can't take a still photo.

The size of the still photo you take while recording a video depends on the size of the video image.

Note:

- You can't take still photos while recording a video in the following situations:
  - If you pause the recording.
  - If there's less than 5 seconds of recording time left.
  - If you set the Movie options to HS movie.
- If you set the Image quality in the shooting menu to RAW or RAW+Fine, still photos will be saved as Fine quality. If you set Image quality to RAW+Normal, still photos will be saved as Normal quality.
- You can take up to 20 still photos while recording a video in 2160/30p or 2160/25p mode. The photos will be saved as Fine quality.

- It may take a few seconds to save still photos after you take them. The part of the video that's being recorded while you take a photo may not play back smoothly.
- The sound of the shutter button clicking when you take a still photo may be audible in the recorded video.
- If you move the camera when you press the shutter button, the photo may be blurry.

Movie Manual (Setting the Exposure for Movie Recording)

In Movie manual mode, you can use the aperture-priority auto or manual setting to control the exposure (shutter speed and f-number) while recording movies.

1. In Movie manual mode, press the MENU button, select Exposure mode from the menu, and press OK.

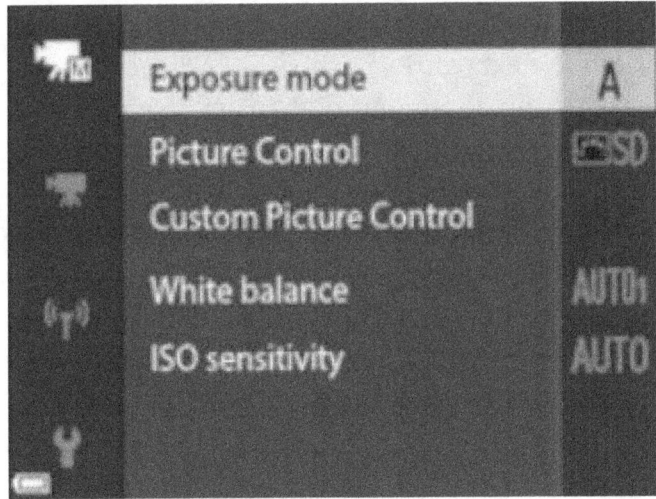

2. Select Aperture-priority auto or Manual, and press OK.

Configure Picture Control, Custom Picture Control, White balance, or ISO sensitivity settings according to the shooting conditions and requirements.

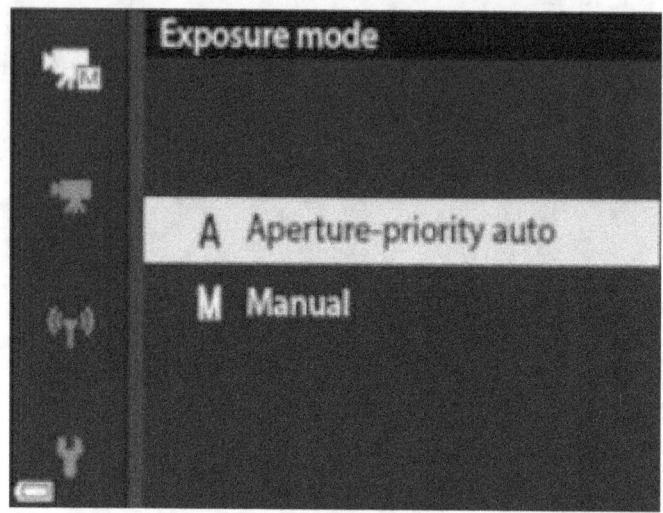

3. Press the MENU button to open the shooting screen.
4. Set the exposure.
   Turn the command dial to set the shutter speed. Turn the multi-selector to set the f-number.

5. Press the movie record button to start recording the movie.
   You can also adjust the shutter speed or f-number during movie recording (except when an HS movie option is selected in Movie options).

   To capture a still image during movie recording, press the shutter release button all the way down.

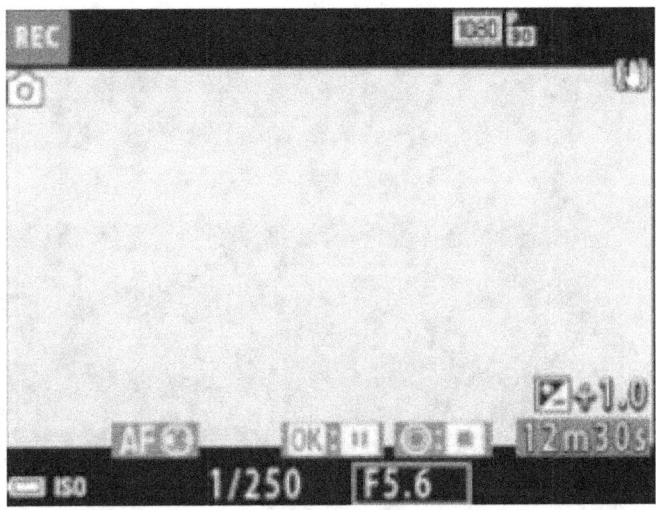

Note: In Movie manual mode, you can't adjust the focus even when you half-press the shutter button before starting the movie recording. To adjust the focus before starting movie recording, set the Autofocus mode in the movie menu to Full-time AF or use manual focus.

Shooting Time-lapse Movies

The camera can automatically capture still images at a set interval to create time-lapse movies that are about 10 seconds long.

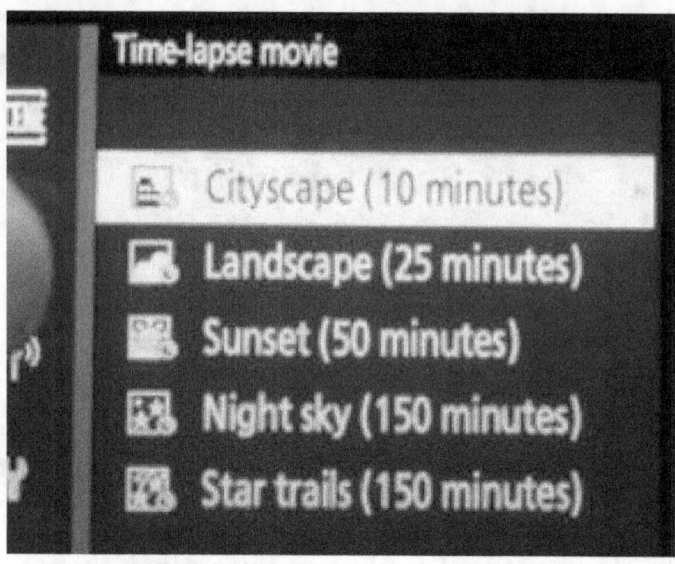

When the Frame rate setting in the movie menu is set to 30 fps (30p/60p), the camera captures and saves 300 images at 1080/30p. When set to 25 fps (25p/50p), the camera captures and saves 250 images at 1080/25p.

1. Use the multi-selector's up or down arrow key to select a type, then press OK.

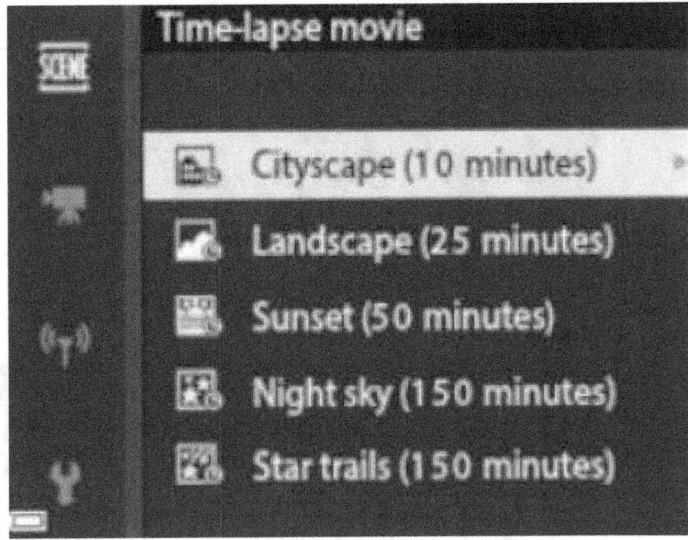

2. Choose whether to fix exposure (brightness) and press OK (except for Night sky and Star trails).

   When AE-L on is selected, the brightness of the first image is used for all images. When the brightness changes drastically, such as at dusk, AE-L off is recommended.

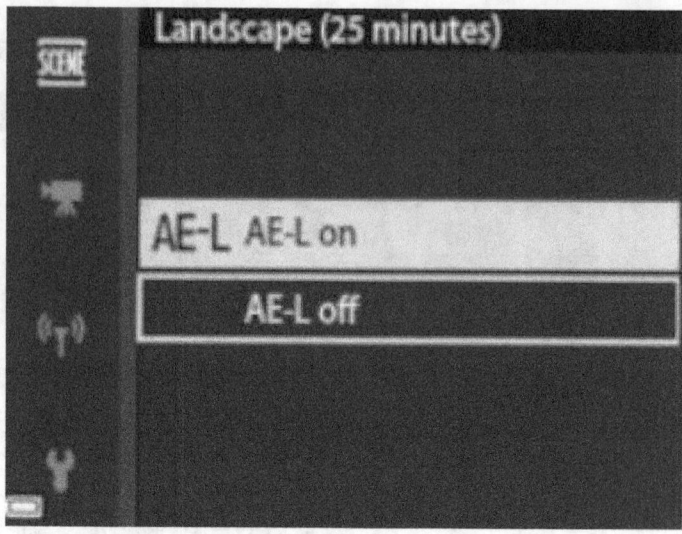

3. Use a tool such as a tripod to stabilize the camera.
4. Press the shutter release button to capture the first image.

   When capturing images of stars, it is recommended that you use manual focus.

   The auto-off function is disabled during shooting.

   When taking star photos, it is recommended to use manual focus.

   The auto-off function is disabled while shooting.

   The shutter is automatically released for the second image and all subsequent images.

   The screen may turn off while the camera is not taking pictures.

Shooting automatically stops when 300 or 250 images are captured.

Press the k button to stop shooting before the set time has elapsed and create a time-lapse movie. Sound and still images cannot be saved.

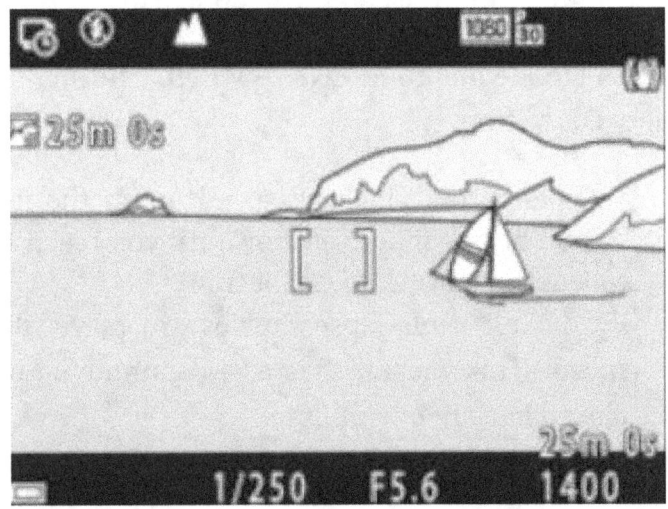

Notes About Time-lapse Movie

- Keep your memory card in the camera until you're done shooting, or you might lose your precious photos!
- Don't let your camera die on you! Make sure to use a fully charged battery before you start shooting.
- Time-lapse movies are special! You can't record them with the regular movie record button.
- Keep the mode dial on the right setting until you're done shooting, or you might lose your photos!

Recording Superlapse Movies

Time-lapse movies are a fun way to speed up time and see the world in a new way. To record a time-lapse movie, simply set your camera to the time-lapse mode and start filming. The camera will automatically compress the time of changes in the subject, so you can watch hours of footage in just a few minutes.

Rotate the mode dial to SCENE > MENU button > Superlapse movie > OK button.

1. To change the playback speed, press the up or down button on the multi selector until you reach the desired speed, then press the OK button.
    By default, time-lapse movies are played back at 2× speed. This means that a two-minute movie will be played back in one minute.

    Time-lapse movies can only be recorded for up to 29 minutes at a time. If the recording exceeds 29 minutes, the camera will automatically stop recording.

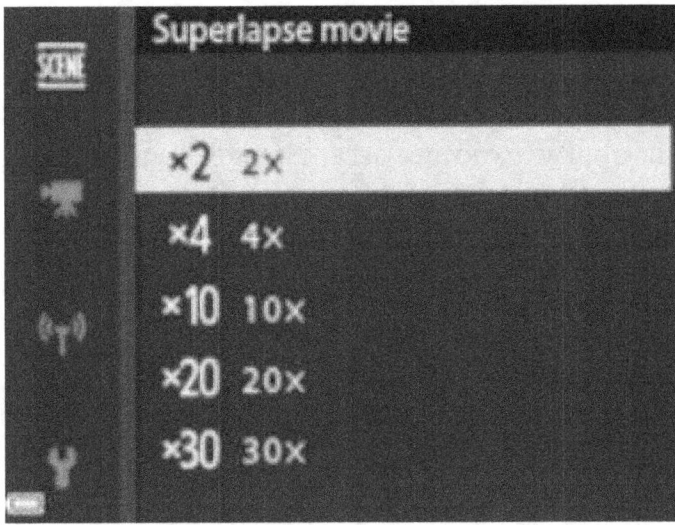

2. Hit the record button to start filming!
   You can check the recording and playback time on the screen, but don't forget to turn on the movie frame so you can see what you're filming! Sound is not recorded, so be sure to add music or sound effects later in editing.

Note: You can take still photos while recording videos! Just press the shutter button before you hit the record button to capture a 1920x1080 pixel image.

CONCLUSION

The Nikon Coolpix P1000 is a remarkable achievement, and its ability to capture decent images at 3000mm sets it apart as a unique product. It has excellent handling, effective vibration reduction, and a clear menu system. However, to offer a camera with such an ambitious lens at a price point under $1000, compromises had to be made elsewhere.

The LCD screen is not the best for a camera with such a high price tag, and much of the body feels like it is made of cheap materials. The autofocus system can work well at times, but it is unpredictable at the focal lengths where it is most likely to be used. Additionally, it is frustrating that the camera locks up after recording just a few shots, even with a fast memory card.

Even with the effective VR system, it is still difficult to compose precise shots at the telephoto end of the P1000's zoom range. Additionally, the image quality at wide-angle could be better.

Anyone serious about telephotography should consider an interchangeable lens camera with a dedicated telephoto lens. These cameras offer better image quality and more control over the shooting process. While it is impressive to see cameras like the P1000 pushing the boundaries of what is possible, it is difficult to shake the feeling that Nikon has overreached itself.